First Edition

Excellence in Business T

Ellen R. Auster
York University

Tina R. Grant
Durham College

Krista K. Wylie
York University

McGraw-Hill Ryerson

Toronto Montréal Boston Burr Ridge, IL Dubuque, IA
Madison, WI New York San Francisco St. Louis Bangkok Bogotá
Caracas Kuala Lumpur Lisbon London Madrid Mexico City
Milan New Delhi Santiago Seoul Singapore Sydney Taipei

The McGraw-Hill Companies

McGraw-Hill Ryerson

Excellence in Business Teaching:
A Quick Start Guide
First Edition

ISBN: 0-07-094562-4

1 2 3 4 5 6 7 8 9 10 TCP 0 9 8 7 6 5

Printed and bound in Canada.

Vice President, Editorial and Media Technology: Patrick Ferrier
Executive Sponsoring Editor: Nicole Lukach
Sponsoring Editor: Rhondda McNabb
Marketing Manager: Kelly Smyth
Developmental Editor: Tracey Haggert
Senior Production Coordinator: Jennifer Wilkie
Supervising Editor: Anne Nellis
Copy Editor: Jim Zimmerman
Cover Design: Sharon Lucas
Interior Designer: Dianna Little
Cover Image Credit: © Steven Hunt/The Image Bank
Composition: Dianna Little
Printer: Transcontinental Printing Group

National Library of Canada Cataloguing in Publication

Auster, Ellen R.
Excellence in business teaching / Ellen R. Auster, Tina R. Grant, Krista K. Wylie.

Includes index.
ISBN 0-07-094562-4

1. Business education--Study and teaching (Higher)
I. Grant, Tina II. Wylie, Krista III. Title.

HF1106.A98 2004 650'.071'1 C2004-901443-9

Table of Contents

Preface

Each of the three of us came to teaching business from a different background and has taught at different business schools. Nevertheless, we each experienced similar feelings as we approached our first class: We felt excited, but also nervous, uncertain, and a bit daunted by the task before us.

Over the years, we also have experienced similar teaching challenges—challenges that we now realize are typical among new and experienced faculty alike, including:

- wrestling with how to design a useful and coherent course;
- deliberating about the most meaningful class content to include;
- muddling as we tried to respond effectively to every student's question;
- wondering what and how much students were learning;
- and worrying about whether we were grading accurately and fairly.

As we faced these challenges and strived to deliver courses that were valuable and relevant, we experimented with various solutions and learned through trial and error how to improve our own teaching. We also talked with our colleagues and asked them for advice about what worked well for them and what did not. However, when we searched for additional resources, we found none geared specifically towards business teaching.

We joined together to write this book because we wanted to fill that gap and to help others find an easier, more efficient path to delivering a successful business course. With this goal in mind, we synthesized and further developed the best of what each of us has learned over the years. We then spent time reflecting, revising, and reworking our ideas, testing them in faculty workshops, coaching sessions, and in the classroom. The result of this process is *Excellence in Business Teaching: A Quick Start Guide.*

Excellence and Beyond—the McGraw-Hill Commitment to Faculty Development, Service, and Support

Superior Service

Service takes on a whole new meaning with McGraw-Hill Ryerson. In addition to bringing you *Excellence in Business Teaching: A Quick Start Guide*, we have consistently raised the bar in terms of innovation and educational research—both in business studies and in education in general. These investments in learning and the education community have helped us to understand the needs of students and educators across the country, and have allowed us to foster the growth of truly innovative, integrated learning.

Integrated Learning

Your Integrated Learning Sales Specialist is a McGraw-Hill Ryerson representative who has the experience, product knowledge, training, and support to help you assess and integrate any of our products, technology, and services into your course for optimum teaching and learning performance. Whether it's using our test bank software, helping your students improve their grades, or putting your entire course online, your *i*-Learning Sales Specialist is there to help you do it. Contact your local *i*-Learning Sales Specialist today to learn how to maximize all of McGraw-Hill Ryerson's resources.

i-Learning Services Program

McGraw-Hill Ryerson offers a unique *i*Services package designed for Canadian faculty. Our mission is to equip providers of higher education with superior tools and resources required for excellence in teaching. For additional information, visit www.mcgrawhill.ca/highereducation/eservices.

Media Technology Services Program

As a component of our *i*Services package, McGraw-Hill Ryerson offers a number of integrated technology solutions for Canadian faculty. These services include content integration, the design of custom test banks or quiz material for online delivery, the design and construction of custom course Web sites in a number of popular course delivery systems such as WebCT, Blackboard, and PageOut, McGraw-Hill's unique point-and-click course Web site creation tool. The Media Technology Services Program also offers specialized faculty training on any solution we develop.

Teaching, Technology, & Learning Conference Series

The educational environment has changed tremendously in recent years, and McGraw-Hill Ryerson continues to be committed to helping you acquire the skills you need to succeed in this new milieu. Our innovative Teaching, Technology, & Learning Conference Series brings faculty together from across Canada with 3M Teaching Excellence award winners to share teaching and learning best practices in a collaborative and stimulating environment. Preconference workshops on general topics, such as teaching large classes and technology integration, will also be offered. We will also work with you at your own institution to customize workshops that best suit the needs of your faculty at your institution.

Research Reports into Mobile Learning and Student Success

These landmark reports, undertaken in conjunction with academic and private sector advisory boards, are the result of research studies into the challenges professors face in helping students succeed and the opportunities that new technology presents to impact teaching and learning.

Acknowledgements

This book would not have been possible without the contributions of many people.

We are grateful to Dean Dezso Horvath for his ongoing support and commitment to the Schulich Centre for Teaching Excellence at the Schulich School of Business, York University, and for his strong personal encouragement.

Thanks to the entire superb team at McGraw-Hill Ryerson, including Rhondda McNabb, Sponsoring Editor; Tracey Haggert, Developmental Editor; Jeff MacLean, Director of Marketing; Joe Saundercook, Vice President Partnerships and Business Development; Nicole Lukach, Executive Sponsoring Editor; Anne Nellis, Supervising Editor; and Jim Zimmerman, Copyeditor. We thank you for sharing our vision for this book and for a thoroughly enjoyable publishing experience.

Thank you also to our external reviewers, Dr. A. Scott Carson, Dean, School of Business and Economics, Wilfrid Laurier University; Richard G. Donovan, Associate Dean, B. Comm. Program, Faculty of Management, McGill University; Dr. Lindsay Meredith, Marketing Professor, Faculty of Business Administration, Simon Fraser University; and Dr. Bernadette Schell, Dean of Business and Information Technology, University of Ontario Institute of Technology, School of Business and Information Technology, who reviewed our book in its entirety and provided thoughtful suggestions and perspectives.

In addition, we want to recognize the many colleagues who shared their insights and experiences. We appreciate the benefit of learning from you.

We are also indebted to Michael Valente for his insight, patience, creativity, and humor throughout the marathon last round of editing sessions on each chapter.

Finally, we each have some personal acknowledgements for those closest to us:

To my mother and father, Don and Nancy Auster, for the inspirational role models you've been throughout my life as both parents and teachers. To my daughters, Lindsey and Shannon, for keeping me laughing and smiling all along the way, and to my husband, Steve Weiss, for Thursday nights to write and so much more. Thank you all for always cheering me on and for your love.

-ERA-

Thanks to Dave, Jason, Melanie, and Trevor for your love and encouragement in all that I do.

-TRG-

Thanks to Em for your love and constant support in all that I embark upon, and to Madeline for your patience, flexibility, and sweet nature.

-KKW-

Introduction

Why You Should Read This Book

Maybe you're new to teaching business and you're looking for some core skills and quick tips to help you become successful in the classroom. Maybe you're a practitioner teaching in the evenings or a Ph.D student soon to go on the market for a faculty position. Or, maybe you're a more experienced instructor looking for some new ideas. Regardless of your position, this book is designed to offer practical tips for accelerating your learning curve and ensuring you are a successful business teacher. *Excellence in Business Teaching: A Quick Start Guide* will help you create a dynamic and valuable learning experience for yourself and your students. It will ensure that you avoid some of the typical teaching pitfalls, spend time efficiently, and focus on the right things.

How to Use This Book

The book is divided into six chapters, each offering guidance, information, and tools for different key teaching activities.

Chapter 1: Pulling Your Course Together offers tips and shortcuts for planning and organizing your course.

Chapter 2: Getting Ready for Each Class provides advice on choosing the content for each class, organizing that content, and planning for in-class delivery.

Chapter 3: Teaching Effectively in the Classroom focuses on how to create an engaging classroom environment that keeps students learning and involved.

Chapter 4: The First Class—An Important Opportunity underscores the importance of this first meeting and shows you how to set the right tone, expectations, and groundwork for a successful course.

Chapter 5: Improving Your Teaching Using Student Feedback presents ideas for obtaining and using feedback to improve your teaching and your course.

Chapter 6: Grading explains how to ensure that your grading is fair and meaningful.

Throughout the book, you'll find key design features that will help you use it as effectively and efficiently as possible. Each chapter starts with **At a Glance**, which crystallizes the key ideas, allows for quick understanding of the chapter, and facilitates the easy selection of topics that may be of most interest to you. Peppered throughout the chapter are anecdotes and examples to bring teaching approaches to life. Chapters are also supplemented with **Samples and Worksheets**, which offer concrete illustrations and practical tools for easy implementation. In addition, each chapter ends with **Frequently Asked Questions** that suggest tactics for addressing situations that commonly arise. Most new business faculty share common challenges, and we're sure you'll find some useful nuggets in these sections too! With this succinct and action-oriented approach, you can choose to read the book from cover to cover or select specific sections that meet your needs and interests.

But I don't have time to read a book on teaching . . .

We know you may be thinking, "But I don't have time to read this book! I've got to start preparing for my classes!" We guarantee that taking 30 minutes now to skim this book and focus on the key ideas in the **At a Glance** feature in every chapter ultimately will save you time, make your classes more successful, and help you to achieve teaching excellence.

Having a strategy for approaching your teaching will also have a significant impact on how students receive your course and how much they learn. Investing some time in getting ready, setting expectations, thinking creatively about course delivery, learning from feedback, and avoiding common new-faculty nightmares will make the entire process a more meaningful learning experience both for you and your students.

How long will it take for me to feel confident in my teaching ability?

Like any new endeavor, teaching your first business course will have bumps and hurdles, which occasionally may leave you shaken and bruised. What's critical is to take the time to learn from those moments, but also to move forward.

How you feel during and after your classes may vary dramatically. You may have wonderful classes where you leave excited, enthused, and raring to teach the next class. However, you will undoubtedly have "duds," where things go poorly and you feel like you are struggling throughout the session.

Throughout these ups and downs, it is essential to remain flexible and responsive. Remember that teaching is a skill that requires continuous learning. Take the time to reflect on your successes and failures and to learn from every class. Consider both the course content and the teaching process as you adjust your approach.

By incorporating the tips, advice, and information offered in this book into your teaching, you should find that you quickly gain increased confidence and enhance your success in the classroom. Over time, as you teach more and more classes, you'll find that you need to pay less attention to the basics of teaching because they'll begin to come naturally. You'll find you have time to think creatively about how best to spark students' interest, keep them engaged, and create the kind of learning environment that they hope for and you aspire to. Before you know it, you'll move from being anxious about each class to eagerly looking forward to this most enjoyable and rewarding experience.

CHAPTER ONE

Pulling Your Course Together

CHAPTER 1 at a Glance

Identify the key learning objectives for your course

- Determine content goals and skill goals
- Review past course outlines
- Talk to others who have taught the course

Build your course content

- Find core course material
- Get supplemental course content
- Ensure course material is practical and applied
- Leverage personal knowledge and expertise

Customize your course outline

- Ensure basic elements of the course outline are accurate and up-to-date
- Make expectations and course policies clear
- Determine the schedule of topics to be covered for each class session
- Use a mix of readings, cases, articles, and current press
- Determine which evaluation vehicles you will use

Take care of course administration

- Order books and/or course packets well in advance
- Reserve all audiovisual course materials and equipment required
- Ensure that your assigned classroom is appropriate

You're probably anxious to get prepared for your first business class session, and chances are you're most concerned about reading the textbook and having the materials ready to present in class. While attempting to balance other time pressures, you might be tempted simply to change the name and phone number on the previous course outline and send it off for duplication. However, taking time upfront to plan and organize your course will create a more enjoyable course experience for both you and your students and avoid lots of hassles throughout the term. In addition, spending time organizing your course will ensure that the course you deliver is relevant and practical, and offers business students the concepts and tools they need for success.

One of the first things you should find out is how much flexibility there is in course design and delivery. If the course you're teaching is a core or required course, you may have limited flexibility. If the course is an elective, you may have a fair degree of freedom.

You should also find out how the course is described in the course calendar. This description is important when pulling your course together because the course calendar establishes student expectations. If you are not aligned with the course calendar, you run the risk of students being disappointed with the course because they thought it was going to focus on different topics.

Identify the Key Learning Objectives for Your Course

Imagine you are at a university function and some business school alumni approach you to share with you why they thought your course was one of the most valuable of their degree. What would they say? This gives you a vision of what you'd probably like to focus in on as you think about the key learning objectives for your course. In addition, there are some specific steps you can take to help you determine what you would like to achieve in your course.

Determine content goals and skill goals

As you think of planning your business course, it is important to consider both content goals and skill goals for your course. Content goals include theories, frameworks, concepts, overarching themes, and concrete managerial examples you think are important to cover. Skill goals involve capabilities that you hope your students will develop through the experience of the course. These skill goals might include leadership, negotiation, managerial decision-making, team-building, or oral and written presentation skills.

In a business school, it's also important that course material be practical and applied. For instance, students in a course on marketing not only should acquire knowledge of relevant theories and concepts, but also gain practice in decision-making, justification of selected strategies, and effective communication of their recommendations. These are the skills they will need to apply marketing knowledge in the business community and make their company's marketing efforts more successful.

Review past course outlines

Department administrative assistants or secretaries often have copies of previous years' course outlines. This is a good way to get a handle on what the course is about, how it has changed in recent years, and where, if at all, there is flexibility for you to customize. For example, you may notice extreme divergence between two former professors' outlines that might suggest there is some room for creativity. In contrast, when outlines from previous years are quite similar or where multiple sections of the same course are offered, flexibility may be more limited.

However, don't assume you need to set aside those innovative approaches you're considering based solely on the outlines. Check with the area or department chair or program director if you've got creative ideas you'd like to incorporate into your course.

Talk to others who have taught the course

An often-overlooked but extremely rich resource of information can often be found by chatting with people who have taught the course before at your school, or colleagues who have taught similar courses at other schools. It is amazing how many good tips you can gain in a 15-minute coffee break with a few of these people. Here are some ideas of questions to ask:

- What do you think students liked most about this course?
- What were the challenges of teaching this course?
- If you had to teach the course again, what would you change?
- Are there topics you would add or eliminate?
- Which testing vehicles or evaluation methods worked better or worse for both you and the students?
- What were the most effective learning approaches you used in the class?
- How much flexibility is there in course design?

Build Your Course Content

In some situations, you may be provided with an abundance of course content, whereas in other instances, you may have to build course content yourself. If your course is quite developed or if your course has little flexibility, you may only be searching for supplemental materials to update and augment previously used content. However, there may be situations where colleagues are less willing to provide information, the course is relatively new, or it may be specialized, as in the case of an elective. When faced with these challenges, building course content may be a primary focus in pulling your course together. Here are some approaches that may be helpful in building the necessary course content.

Find core course material

When building your course content, a good place to start is to locate the core course materials used in previous years. You might also look at similar courses at other schools. This course content can give you lots of fuel for possibilities you might use in your own course. If it's the first time you're teaching a course, the previous year's content can be a good springboard. However, don't feel compelled to use only what's been used in the past unless you know that it's required for the course.

If there is little material to draw upon, then finding a good existing textbook can provide you with a tremendous resource for obtaining the course content you might need. One way of finding these textbooks is to ask your departmental administrative assistant for contact information about local sales representatives for key publishers in your field. Most publishers also have informative Web sites with textbooks organized by major topic. Free copies (called desk copies) may be available to you with a quick phone call or e-mail. You can also research content used in similar courses at other universities to find out what textbooks might work well.

Get supplemental course content

A simple but effective way to quickly and easily augment your course content is to find another textbook on your course topic. While some of the material may be redundant with the textbook you have chosen for your students, you'll find that a second textbook might frame the discussion differently, offer different examples, or provide frameworks and slides that will be "new" to your students.

In addition, check with the publisher of the course textbook you do use for teaching resources, including instructors' manuals, chapter teaching notes, case teaching notes, videos, PowerPoint slides, and other visual aids. Some textbooks even offer online learning tools where students have access to self-graded quizzes, review material, and other interactive exercises.

Ensure course material is practical and applied

Business students demand hands-on, action-oriented content that they can directly import into their careers. While theory and conceptual frameworks offer value, many students will judge the value of your course based on the number of concrete skills they can apply to their job. In order to ensure that your course material is practical and applied, you should extract the key operational and managerial implications from whatever you teach while offering vivid examples of theory and concepts in action. You should also pepper your course with current business events to demonstrate relevance. You may also find that recent business bestsellers related to your course topic can help bring your course content to life. Guest speakers from the business community also can provide excellent reinforcement of "theories in action."

Leverage personal knowledge and expertise

A substantial resource for building course content that is commonly overlooked is your own personal knowledge and experience. Whether you've been working academically or in business in a particular field, you'll likely have more resources on the topic than you might realize. Flip with a fresh mind through old files and materials to see what gems you might bring into your course. You may be surprised how well students respond to content that incorporates your own strengths and experiences.

Customize Your Course Outline

You may be tempted to leap into planning specific class presentations. However, time invested upfront on thinking through and communicating your course outline will save you more time throughout the term. Your course outline will give both you and your students a clear understanding of the goals of the course, course policies, evaluation techniques, class schedule, and other pertinent information. In some schools and with some courses, there may be a standardized template for the course outline that is required. Therefore, you should check with your department chair or program director before spending a lot of time creating a unique course syllabus.

See Table 1-1, **What to Include in a Course Syllabus**, for a detailed description of what you might include in a course syllabus. For an example of how to lay out a course syllabus, see Table 1-2, **Course Syllabus Template**.

Ensure basic elements of the course outline are accurate and up-to-date

An effective outline provides a good summary of the objectives of the course, topics to be covered, and other course policies such as participation expectations, assignment requirements, grading methodology, and how absenteeism and late assignments will be handled. This allows students to plan their workload, prepare for class discussions, and complete graded assignments.

For students enrolled in your course, the course outline forms the basis of a "contract." Since students have a clear understanding of expectations and course policies, the outline also minimizes student complaints and appeals.

If there is no existing outline available, you will need to design your own course and course outline. Start by reviewing the standard components shown in Tables 1-1 and 1-2. In addition, standardized components may be specific to your university or college. Therefore, it is also helpful to leaf through other outlines in your department or faculty to ensure you've included the critical elements required. Once you've developed a draft of the outline, run through all the elements to ensure they are accurate and up-to-date. You may also want to share your syllabus with a colleague to double check that you've got the key bases covered.

Make expectations and course policies clear

The clearer your expectations are from the start, the fewer individual exceptions you'll have to cope with, so you should use your course outline to clarify key course policies. Typical elements you may discuss include attendance expectations, missing or late assignments, make-ups and extensions, plagiarism, and in-class conduct. Although these might seem like trivial or purely administrative details, they are critical for communicating your expectations to your students, and should be reflected clearly in your outline to avoid or minimize hassles later in the term. In addition, clarifying course expectations is important so that students know what they're getting into and can drop the course if they so desire.

Determine the schedule of topics to be covered for each class session

With all the course content that you've pulled together, the next step is to determine the sequencing and ordering of topics. If you're working from a previous outline, this step may be a review and modification. If you're starting with little structure, you may want to use the ordering of topics in the textbook as a guide for determining the sequence of your course. You may also want to refer to the supplementary material or the other syllabi you've collected to obtain additional insights for the course structure. Another aspect to consider is the overarching flow of the course. For example, are you working from macro to micro, from past to present, from theory to application, from simple to complex, or is there an overarching framework that charts the path of the course?

From there, you'll probably want to make folders for each topic and see how much time you want to devote to each, given the content you've accumulated. As you fine-tune the schedule of topics, think about pacing and the processes you'll likely use to teach various chunks of content. For example, if there's some drier theory you want to cover in one class, you may want to mix that up with some more interesting practical aspects of applying the theory in that class or the next one. Finally, consider when heavier and lighter periods are in the term, as you schedule different types of content and various evaluation points. For example, trying to teach a particularly dense and critical aspect of the course during mid-terms may only lead to revisiting it when your students have recuperated.

Use a mix of readings, cases, articles, and current press

As you determine the materials for each class, it is recommended that you integrate other readings, texts, current events, and articles beyond your textbook into the course. This practice significantly enhances your credibility as a professor, and makes your classes more engaging and informative. It gives students the opportunity to see concepts and theory come to life and to apply what they've learned in the text to other sources and real-life examples.

Scan your favorite bookstore for the latest business bestsellers and look for content you can use in class. Stay up-to-date on events reported in the business press and find opportunities to incorporate them into your course outline. For example, an article out of a business magazine might provide a perfect short reading for a mini-case analysis.

In some business schools, cases are also assigned for many, and sometimes all, classes. Cases are an effective method for giving students hands-on practice with managerial analyses and decision-making. Cases are available from a variety of sources. Some textbooks provide cases, either written or video, as part of their teaching resources. Specialized textbooks of cases for a particular subject are also available for some disciplines. Search the Internet and you will find some sites with a variety of cases for classroom use. In addition, some business schools purchase cases from a few case clearing houses. Check with your department chair to find out how cases are commonly ordered at your business school.

Determine which evaluation vehicles you will use

Figuring out the evaluation vehicles you will use and how you will measure success in achieving your goals in a course are another key dimension of pulling your course together. Like some of the other dimensions of the course outline, looking at other similar courses is a good starting point for thinking about what you might use in your own course.

Customizing evaluation methods and assignments is a more complex task. Table 1-3, **Common Student Evaluation Methods**, describes a number of effective evaluation techniques, their benefits, and their limitations. For each technique, guidelines on usage and tips for feedback are also provided. Finally, the table offers advice on when various evaluation techniques are most appropriate, given learning objectives, class size, and grading time availability. In addition, for many of these techniques you can offer students more or less discretion. For example, on an exam, you can offer students the choice of which questions to answer (e.g., "answer 3 out of the following 5 questions"). With group projects, you can require that all students address the same case or issues, or you can allow students to choose topics/companies/cases that are most interesting to them.

You will need to choose which evaluation methods you want to use and determine when each tool should occur in the term. As part of the process of choosing evaluation methods, you may also want to consider:

- Student workload
- The mix of group and individual work
- Whether you want more comprehensive evaluation near the end of the term
- A variety of evaluation techniques to accommodate different learning styles

In addition, you should ensure that the evaluation methods align well with course objectives. For example, if you're teaching a course on negotiation, then the evaluation methods should be assessing negotiation capabilities individually and in groups. Evaluation methods should also align with your own personal capabilities. If you are a strong facilitator, you may want to offer coaching on group dynamics. Similarly, if you're a business executive, evaluating students on their ability to act as members of a board may be a useful evaluation approach.

Take Care of Course Administration

Spending a little time upfront on course administration will prevent nightmares from happening once the term starts. You'll need to take ownership for understanding the administrative processes related to your course and ensuring that what needs to happen actually gets done. Simple logistics can undermine your professionalism. Not knowing that you need a key to your classroom, or that the audiovisual equipment needs to be ordered, or finding out the class has been moved to another room across campus, or not having course materials available will wreak havoc. Don't assume these administrative details will be taken care of for you!

Order books and/or course packets well in advance

Speak with your area administrative assistant about the processes for ordering books and course packets as soon as you find out you are teaching a course. Knowledge of lead times required for textbook orders and course packets can save a lot of scrambling at the time of the first class. Also, find out any procedures for copyright issues for articles and other published material.

Reserve all audiovisual course materials and equipment required

In some classrooms, all the technology you might want as well as flip charts are standard equipment, alleviating some of the burden of getting your class organized. Many classrooms, however, do not have this equipment waiting for you. Thus, you may need to reserve this type of equipment. So, quickly find out how to do this and when it needs to be done. You don't want to arrive in your classroom to find out that it is not equipped with the teaching resources you need.

Ensure that your assigned classroom is appropriate

It's always smart to do a quick check of the classroom to make sure it can accommodate the number of students registered for the course and that it is set up in a configuration that will be effective, given some of the process objectives of the course.

FREQUENTLY ASKED QUESTIONS

How do I figure out what things I have flexibility to change on the course outline and what items are "set in stone"?

Looking at past outlines to see whether or not there is divergence is a good indication whether former faculty members have had some flexibility. It usually comes down to the course that's being taught and the requirements of the program. With required courses, flexibility may decrease, as program administrators need to satisfy fundamental skill transfers to students. With elective courses, flexibility increases because the professor is considered more of a specialized expert and would know how best to teach the subject. However, it's always a good idea to check in with your department chair if you need clarification. In smaller schools you might also ask the program director.

I feel uncomfortable asking faculty directly whether the course has been successful in the past. How can I find out?

Sometimes past student evaluations provide key information. As well, casual conversations with students may offer insight into their perspectives on various courses. In addition, with elective classes, the class number is a good indication of its success, although class numbers can also be affected by the popularity of the field or topic.

If I have the option to customize my course, to what extent should I adhere to previous course outlines and processes?

Although we do recommend you take advantage of the course materials already available, your teaching will be more successful and enjoyable if you ensure that the outline builds on your strengths, interests, and expectations. For instance, if you're teaching a marketing course and you know more about direct marketing than advertising, then you might devote more time to that topic. Similarly, if case teaching is a format you're more comfortable with, then you might tailor the readings for some of the classes to include cases. Again, it makes sense to check in with the department chair or program director to see how much customization is permitted.

There's rarely anyone around when I need some information. Where do I go?

Faculty work different hours and are sometimes not in their offices on a regular basis. If you need some information, try the area administrative assistant for starters, or use this situation as an opportunity to get to know a faculty member whose door is open. If this fails, see the person who hired you. When all else fails, visit the dean's office and they'll direct you.

Is it okay to change my course outline once the term has begun?

Changes to the course outline, once they've already been distributed to students, will come back to haunt you. Inevitably, some students will not be happy with whatever changes you make and you'll run the risk of "breach of contract" grievances.

Some schools may have specific policies regarding changes to published course outlines, so you should check with the department chair or program director before considering any changes.

TABLE 1-1 What to Include in a Course Syllabus

This document provides a description of what should be considered when developing a course syllabus. While a good course syllabus does not necessarily include every one of these elements, you will find that including most of this information will enhance your course effectiveness.

BASIC INFORMATION

Basic information about the course should include: the current year and semester, the meeting time of the course, the course title and number, and location. You might also note any course meetings that are not scheduled for the assigned room.

It's also important to list your name, office address, office phone number, e-mail address, Web site URL, fax number, and office hours. If you list a home telephone number, indicate any restrictions on its use. Include the names, offices, and phone numbers of any teaching assistants or secretarial support.

PREREQUISITES TO THE COURSE

Prerequisites to the course help students realistically assess their readiness for your course by listing the knowledge, skills, or experience you expect them to already have or the courses that they should have completed.

PURPOSE AND LEARNING OBJECTIVES OF THE COURSE

The purpose and learning objectives of the course provide an introduction to the subject matter and show how the course fits within the concentration and program curriculum. Usually called the "course overview," it helps the students understand what the course is about, and the skills, capabilities, and knowledge base they will gain if they take the course. It is useful to give students a sense of how much preparation and work the course will involve.

List three to five major objectives that you expect all students to strive for:

- What will students know or be able to do better after completing this course?
- What skills or competencies do you want to develop in your students?

TEXTBOOK AND MATERIALS

Information on all course materials should be provided. If students need to purchase books or course packets, include information on how to obtain those materials. You should indicate whether the students are required to do the reading before each class meeting. You may also want to provide:

- References on specific topics for more in-depth exploration
- Bibliography of supplemental readings at a higher or lower level of difficulty, in case students find the required text too easy or too challenging.

Supplementary Material. It is always beneficial to provide students with supplementary material to help them succeed in the course. Here are some examples of what to provide:

- Other textbooks or readings
- References on specific topics to acquire additional information
- Glossary of technical terms used in the course
- Online resources that may be helpful to students
- Copies of past exams

E-Learning Course Enhancements. Online learning resources are becoming more prevalent and can be a great complement to traditional resources. Provide information on how students can access these resources, while highlighting the benefits associated with their use.

EVALUATION METHODS

Assignments, Term Papers, and Exams. Evaluation methods should be clearly delineated in your syllabus. State the nature and format of assignments, their expected lengths and deadlines. Underscore how assignments relate to the learning objectives for the course. For examinations, highlight the nature of the exam (essay, short-answer, take-home), topics covered, type of exam (open- versus closed-book), time allocation, dates, and other pertinent details. It is important to inform students in the syllabus whether they will be working in groups or individually for the different evaluation elements they are required to complete. With the group method, it's important to specify how those groupings are formed. You should also clarify how much time students should anticipate spending on reading assignments, projects, group work, exams, or research.

How Students Will Be Evaluated and How Grades Will Be Assigned. Describe the grading procedures for each element of evaluation. Delineate the weighting of each element for the final grade: assignments, term papers, midterms, and exams.

Describe details, such as whether you will:

- Grade on a curve or use an absolute scale
- Accept extra-credit work to improve grades
- Drop the lowest grade, etc.

Class Participation. Class participation is often where grade appeals at the end of the term arise. Ensure that you have clearly outlined both your expectations and the evaluation process for class participation. At a minimum, you should have some record of students' performance for each class. This might include brief qualitative comments or a rating on a scale of 1-5 of their performance for each class, both in terms of quality of participation and quantity of participation.

KEY DATES

Although key dates of exams, assignment due dates, and group work are normally outlined in the assignment section, it is recommended that all key dates important to students be highlighted or bolded somewhere at the beginning of the syllabus. It is recommended that you include on the course calendar the last day students can withdraw from the course without penalty.

COURSE POLICIES

In this section you should clearly state policies regarding:

- Class attendance
- Turning in late work
- Missing assignments, tests, or exams
- Make-ups
- Requesting extensions
- Reporting illnesses
- Academic honesty

You should also include a description of students' responsibilities in the learning process and the professor's and/or teaching assistants' graduate student instructors' responsibilities. You might also establish ground rules for classroom behavior (e.g., Is raising your hand necessary for in-class participation? How will late arrivals to class be managed?, etc.).

ACADEMIC HONESTY

You should clearly delineate institutional policies on cheating and plagiarism. Some universities have information available centrally which you may want to provide. Other times, there may be a standard discussion of these issues that should appear in all syllabi. Check with others at your institution to find out standard practices.

SPECIAL NEEDS REQUIREMENTS AND AVAILABLE SUPPORT SERVICES

Most universities provide resources for students with special needs. For example, there may be special computing facilities or note-taking provided for those with physical disabilities, or audio or visual recording may be available. In addition, many business schools offer assistance with writing, oral presentation, and ESL support. If those types of services are available for your course, you may want to note them in your course outline.

CLASS SCHEDULE

The remainder of your syllabus, which will probably encompass a number of pages, should be devoted to specifying the details of each class throughout the term. For each class session, you should include:

- Topics to be covered
- Preparations or readings
- Assignments due
- Guiding questions for readings
- You might also note other details, such as if the room will be changed or when extra materials should be brought to class.

TABLE 1-2 Course Syllabus Template

XXXXX SCHOOL OF BUSINESS
X UNIVERSITY

MKTG 2000 – Winter 20XX
Marketing Management
Wednesday 1pm to 4pm: Room 300

Professor Jane Doe
Room 303
Phone:
Home Phone: (before 10pm only)
Office Hours:
Teaching Assistants' Office Hours and Contact Information:

Administrative Assistant:
Phone:
E-mail:

PREREQUISITES TO THE COURSE

Students are expected to have completed BUS 1000. The material covered in this course assumes understanding of introductory components of business.

COURSE OVERVIEW AND LEARNING OBJECTIVES

This course examines the managerial problems involved in formulating and implementing marketing plans in business and nonprofit organizations. Emphasis is placed on the importance of buying behavior in influencing marketing decisions. Each element of market responsibility, product development, pricing policy, promotional planning, and relationships with marketing channels is examined. The course develops an understanding of the importance of an integrated marketing program and of the need to relate marketing to other departments within the organization.

TEXTBOOKS AND MATERIALS

List all textbooks and materials used in the course here.

EVALUATION METHODS

Briefly describe all evaluation elements, topics covered, whether work is done in groups or individually, etc.

KEY DATES

Note all key dates.

Paper Outline Due	January 25th, 200X
Midterm Exam	Feb. 16, 200X
Group Project	March 5th, 200X
Paper Due	March 25th, 200X
Final Exam	April 25, 200X

COURSE POLICIES

State course policies on preparation, missing or late assignments, absences, plagiarism, in-class conduct, etc.

Class Schedule *(delineate each class, preparation, assignments due, guiding questions)*

***Class 1** – January 10th, Topic*

Readings:

Questions:

Additional Prep:

------------------ **repeat for all classes** ------------------

STUDENT WORKLOAD

OTHER IMPORTANT DATES

ACADEMIC HONESTY

AVAILABLE SUPPORT SERVICES/SPECIAL NEEDS REQUIREMENTS

TABLE 1-3 Common Student Evaluation Methods: Benefits, Limitations, Guidelines, and Feedback

EVALUATION	BENEFITS	LIMITATIONS	GUIDELINES	FEEDBACK	BEST USED FOR
Take-Home Exams	• More challenging questions • Better method for evaluating students who freeze during exams • Allow for incorporation and synthesis of many concepts	• Rely on student honor system • Duplicate skills required by other large assignments • Lengthy evaluation time	• Be specific on time to spend on exam • State whether students must work individually • Specify the length of exam	• Provide detailed, standard, explicit written feedback to the students • Break the grading down by key elements of the exam	• Integration and synthesis of course materials • Critical thinking questions
Multiple-Choice Exams	• Evaluate simple, factual knowledge • Easy to evaluate for large classes (TAs) • Require best answer	• No process testing • Considered a short-cut by professor • Difficult to give meaningful feedback	• Appropriate for short quizzes on factual course content • Can be one section of a larger exam that includes longer-answer questions • Make clear how they will be marked	• Difficult to provide feedback. You could speak with students privately about the subject matter or about techniques for taking multiple-choice exams	• Short quizzes • As part of a larger exam • Definitions of terms • Very large classes
Group Projects	• Practice group skills and team management • Can assign complex, in-depth projects • Reduce marking • Often useful to supplement with a presentation	• Freeloading occurs • Potential imbalance in skills and capabilities • There may be tensions within the group affecting quality	• Be specific about details of group formation • Be explicit about the grading process • Use multiple sources of evaluation (peer-evaluations)	• Address feedback to the whole group • Use individual feedback either through peer evaluations or through personal feedback • Pay attention to both content and presentation skills • Outline comments for feedback on the presentation as you listen	• Large classes • Classes where future jobs include working within teams (marketing, strategy, etc.) • Classes where presentation skills are required for future jobs
Class Participation	• Enhances student input in class discussion • Facilitates sharing of knowledge • Builds a sense of community within the classroom • Takes some pressure off the facilitator	• Some students may not feel comfortable speaking in class • Students may feel compelled to say something – anything • Requires ongoing in-class monitoring	• Be explicit about how you plan to grade participation • Grade on both quality and quantity of contributions • For students not comfortable, provide	• Make sure evaluation process is explicit and clearly communicated • Provide feedback on quality and quantity. or example on quality: 0 – absent,	• Classes where you want to encourage class participation from the beginning • Classes where student sharing of experiences

	• Enables students to weave in workplace experiences	and grading while teaching the class	other opportunities to speak (e.g., representing their group, responding to pre-set questions)	1 – present but no participation, 2 – said something but comment was obvious, 3 – comment referred to class content, 4 – comment or question that was logical and/or integrated a number of course components, 5 – comment or question was analytical, reflective, integrative, and persuasive. • On quantity, grade on a scale of 0-5 for number of comments	facilitates the learning process • Often not needed in situations where the students are highly motivated to participate (e.g., electives or Ph.D courses).
In-Class Exams	• Quick • Clear indicator of individual performance	• Students' handwriting may be unclear • Some students do not work well under pressure	• Be specific on whether it's open- or closed-book • Use other evaluation methods to balance those poor at exams	• Ensure that you provide detailed comments on the exam • Develop an answer key that outlines the answers • To address common errors develop a grading key where numbers refer to typical errors in the exam	**Open-Book** • Exams with more critical thinking • Large number of concepts **Closed-book** • Where reiteration of material is the objective
Individual Assignments	• Best for students that don't perform well on exams • Can ensure application of most course material • Students can work on a topic of interest and demonstrate creativity • Develop business writing and presentation skills	• Grading is significant • Students may demonstrate breadth rather than depth in concepts because of the amount of material	• Clearly delineate expectations re length • Provide guidelines for selection of topics, and/or feedback on selection • Offer key elements to be addressed if appropriate	• Provide detailed summary comments and page-by-page feedback • Students expect effort in the grading • Comment on writing skills and presentation in addition to content	• Classes where students need to comprehend through application • Times when the topic is complex or difficult to understand

CHAPTER TWO

Getting Ready for Each Class

To achieve the in-class results you want, preparation for each class is essential, and attention to both content and process is important. Specifically, you will need to decide what content will be covered in a given class. You'll want to ensure that the content you choose to use in class reinforces core learning objectives and is interesting and up-to-date. Because you're teaching a business course, you'll also want to ensure you reinforce how that content can be translated into managerial practice.

CHAPTER 2 at a Glance

Determine what content will be covered

- Ensure content covered in class reinforces core learning objectives
- Don't try to cover everything
- Play to your strengths
- Identify a current business event

Determine how content will be delivered

- Select varied delivery modes
- Plan supporting resources
- Design delivery layout

Develop the agenda

- Choose the key topics and activities
- Build a process map

As you prepare for class, you'll want to think in advance about how you plan to deliver the content. Try to use a variety of delivery modes. Things will run more smoothly if you also plan supporting resources ahead of time. Once you've determined the "what" and the "how," the final step is to develop an agenda to keep everything on track, as well as a process map, which will ensure you've considered all the details necessary to make your class successful.

Determine What Content Will Be Covered

Determining content can be challenging. Selecting the topics that are most relevant, deciding how much material to cover, and choosing subject matter that will engage students as business practitioners are some of the factors that must be considered.

Ensure content covered in class reinforces core learning objectives

A first step in class preparation is to identify the key themes and concepts from the material that has been assigned to students for a given class. When selecting the content, force yourself to be explicit about what you want your students to learn in that particular class. Always keep in mind the basic things you really want students to understand and remember, and how you can keep the course relevant to business practice. It's also beneficial to provide students with class content that will help them perform successfully both in the classroom and in the workplace. If you anchor each class in these specific learning objectives, you'll find it easier both to select core material and to frame your key learning points for your students.

Don't try to cover everything

Don't feel compelled to cover in class all the material that has been assigned. Sometimes, you will find that you have more good material than you can possibly cover in a class. In that case, you will need to select what you think is most important to cover. As you think about which topics to cover, you should check in with your department to ensure that the material you're planning to emphasize in class fits well with the objectives of the program. You should also be aware that there may be less discretion in your choice of topics to cover in core as opposed to elective courses.

Other times, you may discover that the readings you assigned weren't so great after all. You might not have enough to talk about and might need to check out the same topic in a supplemental or additional textbook.

Our experience suggests that it is better to cover fewer key topics well than to cover a wide variety of topics in a superficial way. The textbook you have selected is likely to be much more comprehensive than your in-class presentation, so don't attempt to mirror the textbook in class. Indeed, students may get frustrated if you choose to focus only on textbook content, given that they can learn the same material on their own. Instead, highlight and reinforce key themes and learning points, and use examples to bring these key ideas to life.

Play to your strengths

Leverage the business experience and knowledge you have in the classroom. Students gain the most value when they can visualize concrete business applications of course theories and frameworks. Communicating your personal experience and knowledge is an excellent means for making that happen. For example, maybe you can highlight cross-cultural differences in business practice by drawing on a recent business experience you had overseas. Or, maybe you can incorporate key ideas from a speech you've just heard by a leading CEO on recent trends in his industry.

Identify a current business event

By incorporating a current event from a recent newspaper or business magazine article into each class, you can make business theories practical and vivid. This is a great way to establish relevancy and to bring the material to life.

Simple methods for gathering pertinent stories and examples include: looking for examples of the theories and concepts you are teaching in everyday life; scanning business press and daily newspapers; and collecting anecdotes from business people. You might even find the occasional gem in newspaper cartoons or a current pop culture movie, book, or television show. It is a good idea to start a clippings/idea/story file so you always have interesting applications to share with your class.

Alternatively, you can assign specific students to be responsible for presenting current events that are applicable to each class. This allows students to raise topics of particular interest to them and encourages them to keep abreast of current business happenings. Indeed, lots of faculty members start each class with a discussion of "what's in the press this week that relates to our topic of discussion today."

Determine How Content Will Be Delivered

Once you've determined what content will be covered in a specific class, the next step is to determine how that content is going to be delivered.

Select varied delivery modes

There are many different approaches you can use to present material and deliver class content. Some of these will feel more comfortable than others, but try to use a variety of approaches. Using a variety of different approaches for delivering class content will keep your class engaging, interesting, and dynamic. Using multiple modes of delivery also taps into the diverse learning styles of your students and keeps the pace continuously changing. While we often think lecturing is the best approach, lecture-style deliveries are most effective when underscoring key points, recapping key takeaways, and introducing complex material.

In addition to lecturing, there are many other approaches you can use to facilitate student learning. More interactive approaches give you insight into what your students are thinking and how well they are assimilating the information in the course.

If you are new to teaching, you may want to start experimenting with different approaches in a "low key" way to begin with. Using some examples and anecdotes to illustrate concepts and theories is one relatively easy way to liven up class material and increase student involvement. By consciously weaving lots of examples and anecdotes into each class, you demonstrate the application of theory and concepts and offer real-world relevance.

Cases are an excellent way to apply theories and concepts in a specific business context. They allow you to move away from lecture style towards an interactive learning experience that forces students to take the role of decision-maker. In this role, they're required to analyze and understand the key problems, generate viable alternatives, assess those alternatives, propose a recommendation based on the assessment, and develop a comprehensive action plan for the future.

There are lots of other approaches you can try that will also create a more engaging classroom experience. For example, when teaching a case, you can use "class splits" where 1/3 of the class is in the role of employees, 1/3 of the class is in the role of top management, and 1/3 of the class is in the role of customers. Using this type of approach is a powerful technique to help students visualize a business issue from multiple vantage points. Or, you might try a debate and have students represent different perspectives on a controversial business issue. You might also experiment with role-playing and have students step into the positions of different players in an organization to generate discussion. Table 2-1, **Examples of Delivery Modes**, offers a brief description of a variety of delivery modes and highlights when they are most appropriate.

Plan supporting resources

Once you have identified the delivery modes for various components of content, it's important to think in advance about the supporting classroom resources needed to implement that activity. For example, if you plan group break-outs, you may want to bring flip charts and markers for students to record their ideas to ensure easy presentation to the rest of the class. Or, if you've planned to show a brief video clip, book the necessary multimedia equipment.

Design delivery layout

Plan ahead how you will lay out different delivery vehicles. For example, if you're leading a very interactive discussion, it may be best to use flip charts and/or blackboards or whiteboards. In contrast, PowerPoint slide presentations may be most appropriate for lecture segments.

Beyond deciding which resource to use for a given topic, there are also guidelines on how best to lay out the different resources. Always think of the furthest student from the front of the classroom when determining what size lettering needs to be on the blackboard, flip charts, overheads, and PowerPoint slides. For example, when putting up a detailed financial statement, zoom in and/or blow up specific parts of the financial statements to highlight key numbers.

If you're teaching a case, you might want to think in advance about how you plan to use visuals during the analysis. Maybe you want to put key problems and issues on the blackboard so that students can refer to them throughout the analysis. When you're evaluating alternatives, you'll want to lay them out on blackboards, flipcharts, or your screen in a way that they can be simultaneously assessed. Near the end of the case, when the class is beginning to converge on an action plan, you may want to refer them back to the initial problems (that have been strategically placed on the blackboard/whiteboard) so they can assess whether these problems are addressed by the proposed recommendation(s).

Develop the Agenda

Now it's time to put it all together in an agenda. An agenda is a list of 5-10 bullets that conveys where the class is headed. An agenda is useful both for you and your students. For you, it provides a road map for the logical flow of the key topics that need to be covered to achieve the learning objectives for the class.

An agenda is also helpful to the students because it gives them an overview of what's being covered in the class. It also lets them know where they are at any particular point in the class, and it signals to students when it's best to raise issues and questions. In addition, if a student raises a question that you'd like to address — but later on in the class — simply note her name next to that agenda item to prompt you to remember to call on her when you reach that topic.

While an agenda is a useful tool, don't feel that you have to follow it explicitly all the time. Just like a road map, use it so you know where you're headed and what your destination is, but recognize you may stop at some places longer than others or take detours. Try to remain flexible and respond to the mood and the needs of the students throughout the class.

Choose the key topics and activities

To develop the agenda, extract the major topics and themes that best capture both the content and the key activities of a class. For example, as an organizational behavior professor, you may have allocated one class to leadership. Your agenda for that class might include styles of leadership, key theories of leadership, profiles of different leaders, and an exercise that allows students to see their own leadership styles in action. In determining the agenda, think about what's the most meaningful way to structure the class content. For example, you might want to start with a powerful hook that captures students' interest right from the beginning. Then, order your content by moving to theory and then application, moving historically from past to present, posing a question and exploring it, or working through the various dimensions of a framework or model. Try to vary your approach for ordering topics within your classes. See Table 2-2, **Sample Agenda**.

Build a process map

An effective tool for more specifically delineating the key topics and activities and their associated delivery modes is the process map. With the agenda, you have determined the key topics and activities and their ordering. Use the process map to flesh out the plan for the class in more detail. For example, you may want to note the associated delivery modes for each topic and/or activity and the allocated time periods. In order to avoid rushing and running out of time, it is useful to estimate roughly how long each major segment of class material is expected to take. You don't need to stick to this rigorously, but it will give you a helpful guide for managing class pace and help ensure you do not schedule too many activities for the time available.

In addition, you can use the process map to help you keep track of specific visual aids that will be used. Essentially, the process map enables you to visualize the timing and flow of the class prior to its taking place. Table 2-3, **Sample Process Map**, provides an example of a process map and a process map worksheet.

Finally, take the time after each class to jot down some notes on the process map about how things went. The next time you teach the course may be three months or six months later. Thus, it is helpful to document your thoughts about how the class went immediately after class while the details are fresh in your mind.

For instance, the fact that the discussion of transfer pricing took 50 minutes longer than indicated on your process map is an important note to make for subsequent terms. Or, maybe you're teaching a case in a strategy class and groups are responsible for presenting their recommendations on what actions top management should take. You may have found that having ten groups report back for five minutes took twice the amount of time anticipated on your process map. It might be helpful to note on the process map that you'll want to plan specifically for the amount of time group formation and presentation will take in future classes.

FREQUENTLY ASKED QUESTIONS

I don't have time to plan for each class. Can't I just "wing it"?

As the term progresses, you may find yourself overwhelmed with commitments. If things in class have been going well, you might be tempted to "wing it" and forgo the time it takes to put together an agenda and systematically prepare for class. However, our experience shows that structure does not simply emerge without planning. Students likely will pick up on the fact that you are unprepared and may question the purpose of the class or, even worse, may disengage from the class.

How can I determine how much time I need for each class segment?

Use the first time you teach the course as an opportunity to document how long various portions take and how the class reacted to the material. However, while one class can give you a lot of insight, you still may not get the same reaction to the same material from another class. You may also want to check in with students about the pacing of the class with a few open-ended questions that you ask them to respond to anonymously. See Chapter 5, **Improving Your Teaching Using Student Feedback** *for techniques for obtaining student input.*

How can I use cases effectively in the classroom?

Cases can be used to bring together many elements of a course and to improve students' problem-solving and analytical skills. You can have students prepare cases before class for discussion, read cases in class for discussion, or you can use cases as assignments. They are an effective way to make theory practical and to engage students. The more current and relevant the case is, the more they are likely to learn from it.

It is important for you to guide students on the purpose of a case and how it will be used. For example, the purpose of a case might be to illustrate the application of a particular theory in a concrete setting. Communicating the purpose and use of a case allows students to have a clear understanding of the learning objectives and your expectations in order to approach the case accordingly.

You'll find that cases vary dramatically in both depth and length. Long cases often reveal the complexity of real organizational situations. These types of cases present an opportunity for students to:

- *Extract and prioritize key issues*
- *Assess the issues from multiple vantage points*
- *Generate possible alternatives*

- *Evaluate trade-offs between alternatives*
- *Decide on recommended action steps, and*
- *Design a feasible implementation plan.*

Short cases or cases derived from current business press often illustrate a specific theory or learning objective. For example, if there is a Fortune article on a company, you might want to verbally recap the article (with slide support) to demonstrate a "theory in action" and illustrate its relevance. You might also use short cases as a handout in class, having students either observe and comment on theories in practice or formulate an action plan in groups under a time constraint.

Regardless of the nature of the case, you'll find that one of the best ways to prepare for teaching a case is to think of a handful of thought-provoking questions that you can use to guide the discussion. Typical questions that work well for most cases include: What are the problems facing X company? What are the causes of those problems? What are the core competencies? What alternatives might be considered? What actions should be taken and why? How should they be implemented? Once you've had some experience teaching cases, you'll be able to develop more tailored questions pertinent to the given case and class.

Should I be worried that I don't have enough content for class?

Before you assume that you're short on content for a class, check that you're not making assumptions about how easy it is to understand the material. For example, while the "bullwhip effect" in supply-chain management might appear straightforward to you, discussion of that topic may absorb more class time than originally anticipated.

If, however, you've actually allocated too much time for a particular topic, don't assume that's automatically a problem. Indeed, having a little extra class time may provide you with an opportunity to drill down in more detail on a topic, liven things up with an interactive exercise, or provide a much-needed slot of time to review previous material that was challenging for students.

Help! I'm not well prepared for class, what should I do?

There might be a class where you didn't allocate enough time for preparation or where something unexpected happened that cut into your prep time. The best thing you can do is step back, take a deep breath, and don't panic! If you come into class harried and panicked, your students likely will pick up on it and you'll start off the class on the wrong foot.

When you step back, you should focus in on your essential learning objectives, use those to develop a quick agenda, and then try to determine some fun, creative ways to achieve your objectives. For example, this might be the day to break the students into groups and have them work on some issues and report back to the class. Or, maybe you can find some video clips that are relevant and will generate some good discussion. Or, maybe there's an executive in residence or someone you know from the business world who will join you for part of the class on short notice. Or, maybe you come in and ask students to take 10 minutes to review their readings, noting the key takeaways from each reading, which they will then present and share.

Although you can turn this potential disaster into an opportunity to experiment with relinquishing some control of the class by letting students do more of the work, you should recognize that there are costs to being unprepared for class. You run the risk of students falling behind on content, losing enthusiasm, or thinking that not prepping for class is okay.

TABLE 2-1 Examples of Delivery Modes

Student presentations: Enable students to take leadership of the learning process, bring their relevant work experience into the classroom, and hone their presentation skills by encouraging both formal and informal student presentations, some evaluated and some not evaluated.

Interactive learning activities: Ask students to see the world through someone else's eyes by incorporating dynamic learning opportunities into the class.

Cases: Offer real-world relevance and provide an opportunity to connect theory with application through the use of cases. Cases enable students to analyze problems faced by managers, identify key issues, evaluate alternatives, make decisions, and formulate action steps and implementation plans.

Simulation Games: Use simulation games to apply key theories and show cause and effect of managerial decisions in action.

Role-plays: Assign roles to students and ask them to address a specific situation from that perspective.
"Okay, Kim, you be the Senior VP. Chris — you're the dissatisfied employee on your way into the Sr. VP's office to discuss the matter. Chris, what would you say? Kim, how would you respond? Take it away and run with it for about 5 minutes. Now, Chris and Kim, choose someone to pick up your role and continue the conversation."

Debates: Conduct a class discussion where individuals must speak on behalf of their assigned point of view, even if they might not personally agree with this perspective.

"Everyone whose last name begins with A-K, jot down five arguments FOR the proposed regulations in this industry. Everyone whose last name begins with L-Z, jot down five arguments AGAINST the proposed regulations in this industry."*Teamwork:* Give students an opportunity to work with peers during class in order to share ideas and further their thinking.

Class splits: Break the class into groups based on seating location in the classroom and have them analyze an issue from different perspectives. "Left side of the room, you are Michelle X in this case. The center of the room, you are Jack P. The right side of the room, you are Taylor Q."

Group Work: Break the class into smaller groups to discuss an issue or analyze a case. Have groups write ideas on a flip chart while they work and prepare a short presentation to share the results of their discussion with the class.

Pair Discussion: For a quick variation on break-out groups, consider: Think, Write, Pair, Discuss. Pose a question or issue to the class. Have students think about it and write down their thoughts and recommendations. Then have them break into pairs to discuss their thoughts, and have the pairs report back to the class.

Nominal Group Technique: When working in groups, have each person record her thoughts on a post-it note. Then, have each person share her views with the group and place her post-it note on the wall. This allows quieter students to be heard and may minimize groupthink.

Videos and guest speakers: Make your class vivid by bringing concrete examples, real-world relevance, and expertise from the business world into the classroom through videos and guest speakers.

Current events and stories from the week: Improve students' understanding and demonstrate real-world application of theories and concepts by engaging them in discussions of current events and stories from the week that are relevant to the course.

Lecture: Use lecture mode, reinforced with engaging visual aids, thought-provoking questions, and continuous monitoring of student learning, for content that is important to deliver in an uninterrupted form.

TABLE 2-2 Sample Agenda

AGENDA FOR TODAY

- Upcoming Team Projects: Some Things to Think About
- Current Events: What's in the News this Week?
- Overview of Today's Topic and Where We're Headed
- Key Conceptual Frameworks
- Application of the Frameworks: The ABC Case
- Extracting Takeaways from the Case Discussion
- Wrap-Up: Concluding Thoughts and Preview of Next Class

TABLE 2-3 Sample Process Map

TIME	CONTENT	DELIVERY MODE	VISUAL AIDS
2:00-2:05	**SETTLING IN**		
5 min.	Announcements, Administrative Items		
2:05-2:20	**INTRODUCTION**		
5 min.	Review Agenda for Today's Class	Lecture	Flipchart
10 min.	Current Events: Examples from the Business Press	Interactive Lecture	Slides: 1, 2
2:20-3:05	**APPLICATION**		
10 min.	Introduction to Mini-Case	Lecture	
15 min.	Analysis of Mini-Case	Have students work in pairs	
20 min.	Share Analysis of Mini-Case	Solicit ideas from various pairs	Record ideas on flipchart
3:05-3:45	**THEORETICAL BACKGROUND**		
10 min.	Introduction to Theory and Framework: Why It's Important	Lecture	Slides: 3,4 Refer to readings
15 min.	Definitions Examples	Interactive Discussion	
15 min.	Tying Theory Back to the Mini-Case	Ask the students how the theories and concepts tie back to the mini-case	Slides: 5,6,7
3:45-3:55	**WRAP-UP**		

CHAPTER 3

Teaching Effectively in the Classroom

Having great content and a plan for the class is important, but how you deliver that content is what will keep your students showing up to class and staying engaged once the class has started. During your delivery, it is important to emphasize key learnings with an agenda at the beginning of each class and a wrap-up at the end. In addition, reinforcing ground rules for student behavior will help you create an effective classroom

CHAPTER 3 at a Glance

Set expectations early and often

- Articulate and reinforce expectations and ground rules
- Use an agenda as a road map

Emphasize key learning points

- Share learning objectives at the beginning of class
- Reinforce key learnings during class
- End each class with a wrap-up

Involve your students in your classes

- Leverage students' experiences and inputs
- Manage student participation effectively
- Encourage quieter students to participate
- Ensure some students don't dominate class discussion
- Handle weak or incorrect answers with tact
- Respond with honesty to questions you are unable to answer
- Inject energy into the class

Adjust your plan in "real time"

- Consider modifying delivery mode
- Spend more or less time on a class segment
- Adapt when you run out of or have too much time

environment. To keep your classes enthusiastic and energetic, encourage student discussion, vary delivery modes, and, especially in business courses, it is important to bring theory to life with real-world examples and illustrations. Undoubtedly, your classes will not always go as anticipated, so flexibility and an ability to adjust your class plan in these situations will enable you to still create an optimal learning environment.

Set Expectations Early and Often

To achieve a smooth running class, it is essential to establish clear expectations both upfront (as we discussed in the last chapter) and throughout the term. Your students need to understand your expectations about in-class norms, class preparation, participation, and evaluation. Keep in mind that it is easier to lighten up than to toughen up later in the term.

Articulate and reinforce expectations and ground rules

In Chapter 4, *The First Class*, the importance of communicating expectations and ground rules on the first day of class is emphasized. Expectations around class preparation, class participation, in-class behavior, late arrivals, and class absences should be made clear upfront. Be consistent and reinforce these messages throughout the term.

For instance, since student participation is such an important element of many business courses, you need to ensure a climate exists in your classroom that fosters this type of discourse. Early on in the course, emphasize that students must respect one another's thoughts and ideas. Similarly, let students know there is no such thing as a dumb answer or a dumb question. Since there is a certain amount of competitiveness among business students, you will find that establishing the "rules of engagement" early in the term is important to ensure a classroom environment that is considered "safe" and conducive to student dialogue.

As well, it is important for you to model the desired behavior. Be prepared for class if you expect your students to come prepared. Arrive and start on time if you want your students to be prompt. Communicate and deliver on any expectations you set with the students, such as returned assignments, copies of notes or readings, or responses to e-mails.

Use an agenda as a road map

For a given class, it is helpful for the students to have a road map that gives them an overview of what will transpire in class, as we discussed in Chapter 2. A useful way to accomplish this is to walk students through the agenda as part of your introduction to the class. It is important to post the agenda on the board or on a flipchart, where it is visible and can be referred to throughout the class.

Agendas underscore the key learning objectives for the class and demonstrate to students the flow of logic in your teaching and their learning. They also allow you to easily defer good questions to later in the class when the topic in question is being addressed. Finally, agendas keep class discussion focused and on track.

Emphasize Key Learning Points

It is important to emphasize key learning points throughout each class to ensure that students understand the major themes of a particular class and how that class fits into the overall course objectives. In addition, you should take the opportunity to reference any readings or exercises assigned to the students for that class as you teach.

Some simple and relatively easy steps you can take in every class to underscore key learning points for your students include: starting class by sharing the learning objectives, underscoring key learnings as they emerge during the class, and ending each class with a wrap-up.

Share learning objectives at the beginning of class

If you start each class by establishing the learning objectives, students will have a clear vision of where the class is headed. For example, you could start the class by saying, "Today's class focuses on X, Y, and Z. Why are X, Y, and Z important in today's business world?," followed by a short class discussion to gather student input and establish the relevance of the topic. You might also end the introduction with a summary of objectives. "By the end of today's class, we should all have a clear understanding of …"

In addition, highlight any learning objectives that will not be covered specifically in the class but for which the students are still responsible through self-study, readings, or exercises. Remember — the learning does not happen exclusively in the classroom.

Reinforce key learnings during class

During the class, you can underscore key learning points by saying things like, "Does everyone have a good handle on this?...it's critical," or, "You'll commonly see this in practice," or "This is one of the important takeaways from this class."

Using a mini-case, current event, or anecdote from your business experience is another great way to underscore key learning points and make them memorable and "real."

Finally, changing your tone when underscoring a key learning (soft tone is often the most compelling), or reframing a key learning in different ways can also help students understand and recall a topic.

End each class with a wrap-up

At the end of class, it is very useful for students to have a clear understanding of what is important to take away. Allot time for a wrap-up that underscores key learnings, ties any unplanned discussions that occurred back to the course material, and clarifies their relevance. If an agenda item wasn't covered for any reason, communicate with the students about how that topic will be covered in subsequent classes.

Wrap-ups can be achieved in several ways. You can provide a simple summary of what was covered in the class. You can ask the students what they thought the key takeaways were, either verbally or in writing. You could leave students to ponder a key question, which can then be discussed at the beginning of the next class. When short on time, you can quickly refer to existing takeaways on boards, flipcharts, and overhead slides as a means of wrapping up a class, or post them on a class Web site after class.

Some students might be having difficulty with the course content or some may want to explore a topic further. Consider providing directions for either remedial or supplemental materials by highlighting course materials that could be referenced or additional resources or readings that are available.

If you sense a number of students are still struggling with the material, it is always helpful for students to know that you are available for additional assistance, either during your office hours or via e-mail. You may also choose to spend additional time on the topic during the next class or tutorial.

Involve Your Students in Your Classes

Even after you have taken steps to increase student interaction in your classes by using various delivery modes and including examples, you'll sometimes find that students are not as involved in your classes as you might like. There are some easy steps you can take to enhance student involvement.

Leverage students' experiences and inputs

One effective strategy for involving students in your class is to have them share their work experiences or ask them to apply a concept or theory within the context of their work experiences. Don't be discouraged if your students don't have a lot of formal work experience. Part-time jobs, volunteer activities, sports organizations, and relationships with friends and family can provide helpful examples of basic business principles. In addition to increasing the involvement of students in your class, leveraging student experiences broadens the sources of learning in the classroom, increases the relevance of course materials, and is a great way to bring theory to life with real-life examples.

Manage student participation effectively

There are a number of steps that can be taken to manage participation effectively. Before class, you can provide focus questions for students to use as a guide as they prepare for class or offer tips on how they should prioritize readings. These steps will help ensure that students stay on track during class discussions.

You can also post or distribute slides for easy note-taking so that students can focus more on class content and less on taking notes. However, to ensure students remain actively engaged in the class, you may want to provide only key ideas on each slide rather than the full content. Otherwise, students may attend class with minimal attention or skip class altogether.

During class, take time to pause after posing questions to give an opportunity for the more thoughtful or reticent students to raise their hands. Once a student begins to speak, ensure that she is given sufficient time to articulate her thoughts without interruption. As the class progresses, try to provide opportunity for wide participation by ensuring that airtime is not dominated by a few students.

In addition, rather than playing ping-pong with questions and answers by responding to each question asked, play volleyball. Ask the class what they think, or ask others to jump in on the discussion to create an open market for ideas to flow so that students don't always pass the ball back to you.

For example, if a student has just made a recommendation in a case, rather than responding to the student's suggestion, ask the class what they think of the idea. Once other students start contributing their ideas and opinions, stay in the role of facilitator rather than leading the discussion. This means ensuring that students gain the most value out of the discussion by having to work through the ideas themselves, rather than relying on you for the answers.

In the example above, your role as facilitator might be to say, "Let's think about the strengths and weaknesses of that recommendation," or, if another student raises an alternative recommendation, you might say, "That is a great suggestion, but let's finish up our discussion on the current recommendation before we move to another." Then remember to circle back to that student when you're ready to put a new recommendation up for discussion. Some other ideas you might try in order to increase student dialogue are, "Anyone want to hop in the discussion here?" or "What do others think?" or "How can we relate this to the readings?" or "What criteria should we use for evaluating this recommendation?" or "Try to step into the shoes of the key decision-makers. How would you respond to this suggestion?"

Sometimes you may be teaching a class where some students are much more advanced than others. By letting some of the more advanced students take a strong lead in some of the discussions, you often can minimize their boredom. Alternatively, in classes with tutorials, you may find that these more advanced students are willing to assist others who may be struggling with the course material.

Encourage quieter students to participate

Rather than calling on the first person ready with a response, give students time to formulate an idea before beginning the class discussion. This allows the quieter students to become involved. Another approach for reserved students is to let them know in advance of class a question that will be directed to them.

You can also try a method called "Think-Write-Pair-Discuss." Put a question out to the class, ask them to formulate responses individually and write them down. After a few minutes, break them into pairs to discuss their answers with each other. This gives quiet students smaller audiences. If you circulate through the room as these discussions are occurring, you can talk with some of the quieter students about their answers and then ask them if they'd be comfortable sharing their answers with the class. Chances are they will feel more confident because they know that their partner and their professor support the idea they are presenting.

You should also accept that certain people will not speak up in class because of personality, culture, stress, or other personal factors. For those students, you may want to provide other opportunities for them to show you some participation effort. For example, you could set up a one-on-one conversation outside of the class or encourage quieter students to hand in brief case write-ups to demonstrate class participation. Alternatively, online discussion databases can be used to extend the exchange of ideas outside of the classroom.

Cold calling is a technique where you call on students, regardless of whether they have volunteered an answer or not. Done with sensitivity, this technique can be useful in broadening the participant group in a class. In some courses at certain business schools, participation can be given an extremely heavy weighting in students' final grades. In these courses, cold calling is often expected by students.

However, be aware of the risks of cold calling. You might call upon a student and be met with silence, which could put a damper on her participation for the rest of the class and create an awkward moment for everyone. While you can recover from situations like this by moving on to another student or through humor, be cautious when telling students that they have to participate at a given time. As an alternative to cold calling, you might try "warm-calling," whereby you call on a student who indicates he is prepared to answer the question. For example, if you ask a question and establish eye contact with a student who looks ready to participate, you might warm-call him by saying, "Bob, do you have some thoughts you want to share?"

Ensure some students don't dominate class discussion

Students who are very active in class discussions are great when you don't have much to say or are looking for a response to a question, but they can also dominate the discussion.

One approach to avoiding the problem of a handful of dominant students is to always use a hands-up system. Although it's easy to fall into the trap of calling those with their hands up first, be sure to wait for the more reticent students.

If that doesn't work, it is often effective to pull an overly talkative contributor aside. Let her know you appreciate her ideas but that you'd like to get some of the quieter students talking. Reinforce that she shouldn't be offended if you skip over her. During class, you can also signal that you want to hear from other students by saying, "Let's hear from this side of the room" or "Let's hear thoughts from another perspective," or you can even walk to a side or section of the room that hasn't yet spoken and ask if anyone wants to jump into the discussion.

Handle weak or incorrect answers with tact

Weak answers create wonderful learning opportunities because they draw your attention to course content that might not be fully understood by some of your students. Using a weak answer to stimulate a discussion will enable you to judge the extent to which students are struggling with a specific concept and give the class an opportunity to clarify and explore the issue further. These discussions often will benefit everyone, including the professor.

Effective responses to weak answers might include:

- "Can you clarify what you mean by ___________?"
- "How exactly does that relate to this issue/problem/theory?"
- "Can you be a bit more specific?"
- "Can you elaborate on that?"
- "Can you sketch out the logic/reasons underlying what you proposed?"
- "Let's think about the strengths and weaknesses of that idea/approach."
- "What do you think of what was just suggested?"
- "Does anyone want to respond to that with either supporting or refuting views?"
- "Anyone want to build on this?"

Note that not all of these responses go back to the original speaker. Many of them actually draw other students into the discussion and, therefore, take the original contributor out of the "hot seat."

Respond with honesty to questions you are unable to answer

Sometimes you know the answer, but need a minute to collect your thoughts. In this scenario, throwing the question back out to the class often will buy you time and may further stimulate your thoughts. For example, you could ask, "Does anybody else have some ideas on how to approach this problem?"

At other times, you may not know the answer — this is natural. You will gain more credibility as a professor if you are willing to admit to your students that you are unsure, but that you will find an answer before next class. You might want to put the question to the class for input as well, but assure the students that you will come back with a solid response in any case. In this scenario, you could, at the same time, throw the question back to the student, challenging him to research the question as well so that you can compare notes next class.

Finally, there may be times when there is no "right" answer, only better and worse solutions. Helping your students think about criteria for evaluating alternatives is a good strategy in those situations.

Inject energy into the class

Hopefully you are teaching a subject you know and love, and your passion will shine easily. However, you can take additional steps to inject energy into your class and to increase student involvement. Indeed, in today's business school environment, students will expect you to go the extra mile to ensure that classes are not only content-rich, but enjoyable and engaging as well.

One of the most powerful means of accomplishing this is to ensure that your delivery uses a varied range of approaches. For example, you might try group breakouts, pair-wise chats, debates, role-plays or class splits to liven up the classroom environment. You may want to refer back to Table 2-1, **Examples of Delivery Modes**, in Chapter 2, *Getting Ready for Each Class.*

In addition, you can use gestures, movement, and voice modulation during class to add interest and keep students engaged. Avoid the temptation to stay only in the front of the room and instead try to "own the room" by moving up the sides of the room and around the back. Move away from a student who is speaking to increase the student's volume. Move close to cut student chit-chat. Use hand motions to communicate — perhaps a nod to encourage students to continue or a time-out sign to calm a heated discussion. Raise and lower your voice for added impact or effect.

Adjust Your Class Plan in "Real Time"

Sometimes, you will find yourself having to adjust your original class plan throughout a class. Although you'll probably sweat through these kinds of moments initially, you'll find that being flexible and adaptable in the classroom will ensure both that your learning objectives are met and that learning opportunities are maximized. However, if you find you are repeatedly adjusting your plan in real time, you may want to rethink your class planning process. For example, you may decide that you need to rethink your delivery methods, time estimates, or the amount of content you expect to cover.

Consider modifying delivery mode

While it is important to have an agenda for each class, you'll discover that flexibility will allow you to be responsive and to adjust your class plan as needed to maximize learning opportunities. Being flexible does not mean abandoning your agenda — it simply means you might achieve the learning objectives of the session differently than you had anticipated.

For example, if you're not getting any response from a class discussion, try breaking students into groups and having them report back to the class. Or try pair-wise chats with students to share ideas with each other for a few minutes and then ask them what ideas they generated. If students can't think of concrete illustrations for a concept or theory, try giving them some detail from a current business event and let them put the pieces together. Or, engage them with a vivid story of one of your own business experiences.

If class is at a standstill, you also can ask your students if something in particular is inhibiting their participation. Sometimes, it may be that the way you've framed a question is confusing. Or, it might be the nature of the content, the hour of the day, or the fact that it's mid-term week. You may also want to think about calling break a bit early to regroup your thoughts and reset the tone of the class.

Spend more or less time on a class segment

While we encourage you to run an organized class, your class plan does not have to be rigidly adhered to. Effective teaching is also about being able to adjust the plan on the fly to accommodate class dynamics. For example, you might choose to spend more time than you had planned on a class segment if students are very engaged and "eureka" learning moments plentiful. Alternatively, if students are worn out, you might choose to shorten that segment and shift gears to a more engaging topic, circling back at a time when the class has more energy.

Adapt when you run out of or have too much time

It is likely that at some point during the term, you'll forget to check the time and suddenly realize you only have 10 minutes left to cover 45 minutes of material. In situations such as these, honesty is the best policy. Tell students "the class was so engaging that it seems we've lost track of time." Although your inclination may be to rush through the remaining material, cover what you can at your usual pace, do your wrap-up, and start where you left off in the next class. You also could consider posting some material on your course Web site if you have one.

Alternatively, there may be situations where you've covered all the content you planned for a class but there are still 45 minutes remaining. This extra time provides a great opportunity to take some of the more challenging content from that class and weave in some of the more time-consuming delivery modes such as debates and group breakouts. Although 45 minutes may seem like a long time, you'll quickly realize that the process of running a debate or group breakout can easily consume 45 minutes or more. Another tactic for coping with excess time is to solicit student feedback on any aspect of the course (delivery, lecture style, evaluation, content). A third option for absorbing extra class time is to provide students with the opportunity to work on any group projects they have been assigned for the course. Finally, if other classes in your course ran over the allocated time, this might be an opportunity to end class early and give students the opportunity for one-on-one discussions with you, if needed.

FREQUENTLY ASKED QUESTIONS

My students seem bored and uninterested. What am I doing wrong?

*Keeping your enthusiasm up when your students seem bored and uninterested is one of the toughest teaching challenges. For easy ideas on getting your students more involved and engaged, try some alternative delivery modes such as pair-wise chats, role plays, group break-outs, or debates. See Table 2-1, **Examples of Delivery Modes**, in Chapter 2, Getting Ready for Each Class, for additional ideas and details on delivery modes.*

If you try to jazz things up in the classroom and still find the students to be less involved than you had hoped, consider the possibility that there may be alternative explanations for their behavior. For example, students are notorious for being tired during mid-term week, and tend to be preoccupied and occasionally skip class during recruiting seasons. During these weeks, it may be helpful to show that video you had planned or even to give them a few minutes to review a case before launching into a case discussion. Their level of preparation for your class will also be impacted by the workload in other courses they are taking. In short, by being sensitive to the students' frame of reference, you may uncover other reasons why your classroom experience is not working as you had hoped.

In the class I'm teaching, participation is not graded and students are not responding when I ask questions. How do I create some discussion?

In addition to trying a variety of delivery modes (e.g., pair-wise talks, debates), sometimes all you need is a few people to start talking to change the atmosphere or class culture. Subtle body language of students often can provide indicators of a willingness to participate. For example, students who sit upright, raise their eyebrows, or even smile a bit may provide the cue you need to engage them.

Another tactic for creating discussion in the classroom is to present a controversial business event and ask students for their opinion. The closer a story is related to the students' interests, the greater their willingness to participate and get involved.

How do I deal with diversity in the classroom?

Many schools have strong international initiatives and are proud to have students and faculty from around the world. Therefore, it is likely that you will teach a diverse class and that you will find that many of your students do not share the same first language with you or with one another. While diversity clearly adds to the learning of any classroom, it can also pose challenges for effective communication.

There are several strategies you can use to optimize learning in a diverse class. Ask students to repeat or clarify their point if you don't understand what a student is saying. This approach ensures that you do not skip over their contribution or question and that the other students in your class understand the point being made and have the opportunity to learn from their peers. If you still can't understand a student after she has repeated her point, try having another student clarify, apologizing for your inability to hear/understand. Over time, you'll find that once you hear a student speak on multiple occasions, it will become easier for you to understand her.

In addition, when using Western products or businesses as examples in your lecture, ensure that you don't assume everyone in the class is familiar with the product or way of doing business. Provide an appropriate description and background information so everyone can understand your point.

Finally, diversity does enrich learning by offering multiple viewpoints and experiences. Take advantage of those learning opportunities. For example, you can ask how an issue would be handled differently if it were taking place in other countries.

How should I handle an offensive comment in the classroom?

Inevitably, awkward moments, such as offensive comments, will arise in the classroom, and you need to find your own personal approach for handling these situations. One challenging awkward moment occurs when a student makes a comment that could be perceived as sexist, racist, or insulting in some other way. Depending on the significance of the comment, and how clearly it is offensive, your response may vary. For example, if you are unsure about how to handle this type of situation and it is somewhat unclear as to whether it is offensive, you might simply rephrase the comment and move on, drawing no more attention to it during the class.

Another approach would be to say you feel that the comment is inappropriate and then move on. However, with either of these approaches, you should take the time after class to pull the student aside and raise his awareness about the issue and clarify classroom norms about appropriate and inappropriate comments. A third approach is to allow a conversation to develop about the issue and have the class learn from the issue, steering the attention away from the person who made the comment, and using the opportunity to clarify appropriate classroom behavior with the entire class. In the worst of situations, a student may be repeatedly offensive to others in the classroom. Most colleges and universities have resources and processes in place for dealing with these extreme cases.

We're a few weeks into the term, and I'm finding that students are showing up late to class and not returning promptly from breaks. What can I do?

The best tactic is to ensure that you always arrive on time and always start the class when it is scheduled to begin, regardless of how many students are in the room. This will send a strong signal that you're not going to lose valuable class time just because some students are late.

Also, students tend to pick up on the energy level in the room. If you enter the classroom enthusiastic about the course material and fired up about the subject and about teaching the students, students will not want to "miss anything."

Should you find yourself late on any occasion, apologize to the class and reiterate that being on time is important for everyone, including the instructor!

To manage break schedules, make sure you tell students how long the break should be and state a specific restart time. For example, you could say, "We'll take a 15-minute break. My watch says 3:00 now, so please be back by 3:15."

You should resume teaching at the time you indicated. A quick signal to those standing around outside your classroom right before you resume is sometimes useful. For example, you might say, "OK, everyone, we're going to dive back in now..." However, do not wait until all the students have returned from the break. If you wait for all of your students to return before starting to teach you will find that breaks will get longer and longer.

If lateness persists with a number of students, try finding out whether there's a reasonable explanation for the occurrence. For example, maybe these students are late for class because they are taking a course prior to yours on the other side of campus. Or, students may be late returning from breaks because of the limited washroom capacity or because of the lineups at the closest coffee shop.

4

CHAPTER FOUR

The First Class—An Important Opportunity

The tone and expectations you establish in your first class are important elements of a successful term. Like any other human encounter, first impressions in teaching are important, and it can be difficult to recover from a foul-up. Your image of professionalism is impacted by how you introduce the course you are about to teach and can be disrupted by some

CHAPTER 4 at a Glance

Introduce yourself

- Give your students some background information
- Explain your availability outside of class

Outline the major themes and learning objectives

- Highlight course objectives
- Emphasize skill objectives of the course
- Build enthusiasm for the course

Set clear expectations and ground rules

- Set expectations for in-class behavior
- Review the course outline, assignments, and grading
- Discuss policies for late submissions and absences from class
- Set expectations for on-time class starts and returns from breaks

Avoid administrative mix-ups

- Bring copies of the course outline
- Understand how students' course materials are purchased and distributed
- Bring a current class list and know drop/add and waiting list procedures
- Have the classroom materials and resources that you need
- Know your classroom and whom to contact to resolve problems

Get to know your students

- Student introductions
- Student profiles
- Name cards
- Student pictures

fairly minor administrative issues. Your first class is pivotal to the success of the course and, as such, deserves your utmost attention. Introductions, highlighting course objectives, expectations, and ground rules upfront, as well as taking care of administrative details are all key components of any successful first class. Depending on the course size and format, getting to know your students is another potential key element.

Introduce Yourself

As noted already, first impressions are important in getting your course off to a good start. With this in mind, take some time early on in the first class to ensure you introduce yourself to your students and let them know your availability outside of class.

Give your students some background information

Students are often interested in finding out about our backgrounds, experiences, and even a few tidbits about our life beyond the course! A brief and light personal introduction provides an opportunity for you to establish credibility and rapport. You can use this introduction to establish credibility by sharing with the class your academic and work experiences spun in an interesting and creative manner. When establishing rapport, you may want to share a story that reminds the students that your life is more than what they see in the classroom. For example, if it's the beginning of the fall term you may share a humorous story that happened to you during the summer or you may share some thoughts of what was running through your mind on your way to class. You should also write the course name and number on the board to alert students that might be in the wrong class.

Explain your availability outside of class

In the first class, you should let students know how they can reach you outside of class. A common practice among high-performing teachers is the dedication of time and support to their students. Indeed, most instructors probably underestimate how much students appreciate being able to talk and discuss issues with their instructors outside of class.

Having office hours at the school is essential. Let your students know when you will be on campus and if you encourage drop-in visits or prefer appointments. You should also provide students with e-mail and voice mail contact information. Although crucial for all instructors, this is especially important for part-time faculty, who may spend less time on campus. This also applies to instructors teaching online courses. Let your students know your typical turnaround time for responding to both e-mail and voice mail. For example, you may want to stipulate that voice mail will be returned within 24 hours and e-mail within 2-3 days.

Outline the Major Themes and Learning Objectives

It is important to introduce the major themes and learning objectives of the course in the first class. This introduction provides students with a clear idea of what the course is about and allows them to assess whether the course aligns well with their academic aspirations. If it is an optional course, they can determine if the course is a good fit with their objectives and if they are interested in staying enrolled.

Highlight course objectives

Right from the beginning, it is very useful to the students to have an overview of the course and to have a clear understanding of how various sections of the course build towards overall learning objectives. If possible, develop an overview framework or schematic that captures the key themes of the course. You can use this framework to review the outline and show how the course achieves the learning objectives. You can also use this framework to demonstrate where the key topics fit into the overall picture of the course. If you refer to this overall framework throughout the term, the students will understand how individual classes fit into the overall course and how class topics interconnect and relate to the course objective. Refer to Chapter 1, *Pulling Your Course Together*, for additional ideas on developing course objectives.

Emphasize skill objectives of the course

In most business courses, there are learning objectives beyond the course content, which might include the development of analytical skills, oral presentation skills, articulating ideas to others, working effectively in teams, or business writing. These additional objectives are also important to highlight in the first class as further takeaways from the course.

Build enthusiasm for the course

To build students' enthusiasm for your course, ensure that in the first class you don't do all the talking. Even though there are many administrative tasks you'll need to cover, take some time to engage your students through a discussion of current events, a mini-case, or an experiential exercise that illustrates and brings to life the key themes of the course. Dedicating time in the first class for some interactive activities that get students involved helps set the tone of the course, builds enthusiasm, and also enables you to get a sense of the class dynamics and of student knowledge and experience.

Set Clear Expectations and Ground Rules

Your first class is an important opportunity to set expectations and ground rules. Since every action sets a precedent, it is important to get started on the right foot and, as we discussed in Chapter 3, it is much easier to "start tough" than it is to tighten up expectations later in the term. If appropriate, you can relax the rules as the course progresses. Some of the topics you likely would address in the first class include the following:

Set expectations for in-class behavior

The tone of your entire course can be impacted by how you set expectations regarding in-class behavior in your first class. The importance of setting expectations is also discussed in Chapter 3, *Teaching Effectively in the Classroom*. With this in mind, clearly articulating the "rules of engagement" and modeling the behavior you expect from your class are key. For instance, if it is important to you to encourage a lot of class discussion, stating this expectation upfront and providing opportunity for class participation right from the very first class are important. If having students raise their hands to contribute is important to you, then, again, it is important to let students know this and to adhere to this "rule of engagement" right from the very first class.

Review the course outline, assignments, and grading

In many cases the students will not have reviewed the course outline prior to the first class. It is recommended that you take the time to review the outline in detail and to highlight any specific requirements and expectations you have.

Review key expectations, format, due dates, and other pertinent information for each assignment. Since students are balancing a number of courses, workload, and deadlines, it's unwise to change the outline once the course has begun. Significant changes can cause student backlash. At some academic institutions, the course outline serves as a contract between the professor and student, which can only be changed if everyone in the class agrees. At other institutions, there is more flexibility. Be sure you are aware of how your institution views course outlines and communicate this to your class.

Students should have a very clear understanding of the grading processes for your course by the end of the first class. Students tend to be very focused on their grades, and you'll save a lot of time and hassle throughout the term if your evaluation methods are clearly articulated upfront. This may include specification of guidelines for student preparation and study. It should also include reiteration of school policies around exams and evaluation. Finally, provide as much detail as possible about your grading process, including who's doing the grading (i.e., you or teaching assistants), grade distributions, and type and nature of feedback. See Chapter 6, *Grading*, for a more detailed discussion of these issues.

Discuss policies for late submissions and absences from class

You should establish a clear and consistent policy for dealing with late submissions. Since variable due dates raise equity issues for students handing in assignments on time, late submissions should be discouraged. If you are prepared to accept overdue assignments, penalties for late submission should be discussed.

Absences from class should be discussed as part of your review of class participation processes and grading. Due to the interactive nature of many business classes, missing class normally will impact class participation grades.

In addition, you may want to specify expectations about class absences. For example, you may want to be e-mailed prior to the class. You may also want to give students missing a class for legitimate reasons (illness, job, etc.) an opportunity to hand in a "class-absence" write-up. See Table 4-1, **Example of Classroom Absence Guidelines**.

Set expectations for on-time class starts and returns from breaks

In the first class, it is important to arrive on time yourself and to begin class on time in order to set the expectation that drifting in late is unacceptable. In addition, you may want to underscore that for optimal classroom effectiveness, everyone is expected to be at class on time.

For long classes (e.g., 2-3 hours), you should plan a class break at roughly the midpoint of the class. Breaks are typically 10-15 minutes in duration, but check the norms of your program. When announcing the break, be explicit about the return time, using the clock in the classroom to ensure everyone returns at the same time. When the break is over, resume class promptly to send the message that breaks will start and end as scheduled.

Avoid Administrative Mix-ups

There are some annoying administrative details that can make you look unprepared and unprofessional if they are not handled properly. There are also some common questions and issues that often arise during the first class. You will find it worthwhile to anticipate some of these administrative problems and issues before the first class so that when they occur, you can handle them effectively and minimize class disruption.

Bring copies of the course outline

You want to ensure that all students have a copy of the course outline for reference when you introduce your course. Not having copies will bring the class to a grinding halt, so make sure you have a copy for each registered student as well as a few extras for additional students who may attend the first class.

Understand how students' course materials are purchased and distributed

Students will be asking you for information about how to obtain your course materials during the first class, so it is well advised to understand the distribution process at your school. At every university or college, the process for obtaining course materials is different. For example, some schools have students purchase materials through on-campus bookstores, while other schools have fees built into tuition so course packets are distributed in class.

Additionally, if you are using any materials from your course packet in the first class, don't presume that all students have obtained the packet and have remembered to bring it to class. Bring copies of any materials that you are going to refer to in the first class.

Take the current class list and know drop/add and waiting-list procedures

Frequently, students will look to you as someone who can help them with school procedures regarding dropping or adding the course or managing their position on a waiting list. Although you might not want to get involved in these administrative issues, it is important that you familiarize yourself with the policies before the first class.

There are some easy steps you can take to prevent the registration process from becoming an issue. First, you should obtain the latest list of students registered for your course and take attendance in the first class so that you have a record of who attended.

Second, you should familiarize yourself with the drop/add and waiting list procedures at your school. Some things you need to find out are time frames of the processes, who is involved, and how they are administered. For example, if the course you are teaching is either popular or required, you may have students waiting to get in. If you find out that you are in charge of the waiting list for your course, you'll need to establish decision rules for deciding which students get in. For instance, is it first-come, first-served, or by concentration or major, or by student seniority?

Have the classroom materials and resources that you need

It is easy to miss the basic tools you need to teach. Don't presume the class will be fully stocked with the technology you need, markers, flipcharts, and nameplate cards. As soon as you know the classroom you're teaching in, you should ensure that it is compatible with your technology needs. If you need additional resources, you should contact your area secretary as early as possible, since securing these resources normally requires significant lead time. Having your own "emergency kit" filled with necessary materials will prevent you from wasting valuable class time. See Table 4-2, **First-Class Checklist**, for a comprehensive list of what to consider before your first class.

Know your classroom and whom to contact to resolve problems

Administrative mix-ups can waste time and cause frustration for you and your students. Therefore you should take the time to visit your classroom prior to the first class. Use this opportunity to become familiar with the layout of the classroom, to test classroom acoustics, and to check that the ordered technology is present. This first classroom visit also may reveal other glitches that might undermine your ability to teach the first class effectively. For example, the classroom may be too small for the size of your class, or you may be missing markers and flipcharts. See Table 4-2, **First-Class Checklist**, for a list of questions you may want to ask and reminders of what you may want to bring for your first class.

Get to Know Your Students

Since a key component of most business courses is student involvement and participation, getting to know your students is important. Some of the suggestions in this section are dependent on the size of your class, the format of your course, and the resources available at your institution. However, your students will greatly appreciate any steps you can take to develop rapport with them and facilitate discussion in the classroom.

Student introductions

If class size permits, having the entire class introduce themselves by stating their name and a few other facts about themselves is one effective icebreaker for the first class. Student familiarity with one another will vary from class to class so it's always a good idea to have students briefly share background information. Introductions are particularly helpful if the students are expected to form working groups within the class. Be creative and think of prompting questions that both break the ice and allow people to provide information that might be pertinent to the class. For example, you could ask, "Who is the business leader you admire most and why?" or, "Twenty years from now, where would you like to be?" For elective courses, you might ask why students chose to take the course or what they are hoping to learn from it. You could have each student share this information with the entire class or have students discuss in smaller breakout groups.

Another effective first-class icebreaker is to have students share information about themselves in pairs, using a list of questions. Each student would then introduce the other sharing her interests, work experience, and other pertinent information such as why she chose to enroll in the course.

Student Profiles

For facilitating an engaging classroom discussion, information about students' previous work experience, educational background, subject major, and career objectives can be helpful. You can use this information to understand class composition, and it may also be beneficial to bring this information into classroom discussions. For instance, knowing that many students have worked in the banking industry may provide excellent insight into how to prepare for and deliver a case related to that industry. If you don't have access to information about student backgrounds through your school, you can collect it directly from the students. A simple approach is to hand out a quick information form such as the one shown in Table 4-3, **Sample Student Information Card**.

Name cards

Most business schools provide nameplates for their students. Having your students bring their name cards to every class will help you get to know your students and help them get to know each other. Let them know about this expectation during the first class. You may also want to bring markers and cardboard nameplates to class for the inevitable times when a student forgets his official nameplate.

Student Pictures

As obvious as it may seem, part of creating a comfortable class environment is to know students by name. Being able to call students by name in the classroom or in the hallways may be more important to them than you might realize. Learning to match a name to a face is made easier by having student pictures on file.

Your school may have student pictures online. Alternatively, you can take a photograph during the class break. Remember to write their names down or have them hold their name cards during the picture so you know who they are when you get the pictures. One effective method for quickly memorizing student information and being able to visually recognize them is to staple student pictures to the back of student information cards. It's recommended that you flip through them during any spare time you may have during the first few weeks so you can get to know your students quickly.

FREQUENTLY ASKED QUESTIONS

I have a lineup of students asking me to sign forms to enroll them in my class. I am not familiar with the school's policy on adding or dropping a course. What should I do?

Every school has its own policy on dealing with student enrollment in a course. Many factors such as prerequisites, room capacity, or wait-lists must be taken into account. Rather than commit on the spot, you should tell students you'll e-mail them within 2 days and get some guidance from the school.

The textbook and course kit are sold out, and several students are without the necessary course materials. I want to help them so they can be prepared for class but am not sure how to handle the situation.

Before the course begins, make all course materials available in the library in Reserved Readings. This is helpful if course materials are in short supply or for students who can't or don't wish to purchase materials. This will prevent students coming to you to borrow copies of texts or readings.

If the course has already begun and you've run out of course materials, have your area secretary order additional materials. In the meantime, you should make additional hard copies to be distributed in class for the first few weeks of the course.

The students are very noisy at the beginning of class and I'm standing there waiting to start. How can I let them know I want to begin?

Good indicators that you are about ready to start: "Okay...I think we'll get started now" or "Even though a few people are still straggling in....we'll begin now." Then say, "This is XXX course and I'm Professor Y" to signal to students that they should stop talking because class is about to begin. You could also turn off and on the lights a few times to get the students' attention.

Do I tell them this is my first time teaching? Will they "go for the jugular" or cut me some "slack"?

Although you probably won't tell the students that it's your very first class teaching, you may want to say that you're a relatively new professor at the school. When you face challenges that are inevitable in your first term of teaching, many students will be more understanding and helpful. However, some students may challenge you more and some may resent having a "rookie." For those students, you may need to work harder to establish credibility and authority.

How do I deal with a student who challenges my authority in the first class?

Sometime in the first few classes, you likely will have a student who challenges what you are doing or saying in an aggressive way. For example, she might say something like, "From my experience in X industry, this is not true." Try not to get defensive and try to pull the class into the discussion. For example, you might try tossing the question back to the class. You might say, "Can we hear from some others on their experiences?" or you could try breaking down the question. For example, "Do we think that this might be more applicable in some industries than others?" In short, try to avoid a battle between the student and yourself and try to diffuse the discussion.

I planned some group projects for the course. Should I set up groups during the first class?

In most schools, there will be some changes to your class roster within the first class or two. This lack of stability in the class roster can cause disruptions if study groups or teams for projects are established in the first class. Consider waiting until the second or third class to form groups.

TABLE 4-1 Example of Classroom Absence Guidelines

CLASS ABSENCE WRITE-UPS

If you must miss a class for a **legitimate** reason, and you want to attain class participation points (maximum of 5 points for both quality and quantity), the following process must be followed:

- Let me know **in advance** that you will be absent from the class and why. At the latest, this means before class starts at 2:30. (555-5555 X555)
- Write-up should be 3-5 pages long.
- Write-up should include:
  - Analysis of the case(s), if there is a case assigned
  - Responses to guiding questions (if listed)
  - If there is not a case of guiding questions for that week, write up something interesting and relevant to that week's readings.
- Write-ups will be due by the end of the missed class, **no later than 5:30 p.m**. (e-mail is jdoe@bus.university).
- Total possible points attainable will be 5 for quality, and 5 for quantity. Your hand-in will be graded on a scale of 1-5. That grade will be entered into the class participation scheme for both quality and quantity.
- **All policies noted above must be met to attain points.**
- You may only exercise this option twice (max!) in the term.

TABLE 4-2 First-Class Checklist

INFORMATION TO KNOW:

- ❑ What technology is available, what technology must be ordered, and how do I procure this equipment?
- ❑ What are the student drop/add procedures and regulations? What is my role and authority in this process? When will my class list be finalized?
- ❑ How do students go about purchasing and/or picking up course materials?
- ❑ Have I made all course materials available in the library?
- ❑ What is the student access to e-mail and other computing services?

CLASSROOM CHECK:

- ❑ Do I know the location of the classroom?
- ❑ Is the classroom compatible with the technology that I'm using?
- ❑ How will I organize furniture and/or students in the classroom to accommodate my chosen delivery modes?
- ❑ Are there markers, flipcharts, and other required teaching tools?
- ❑ Can I operate the classroom equipment, lights, screens, etc.?
- ❑ Who is in charge of the physical aspects of the building I teach in and how do I contact him in case of any problems?
- ❑ Will the door to the classroom be locked?

WHAT TO BRING:

- [ ] Extra overhead markers, tape, slides, power and extension cords, chalk, pen and paper
- [ ] Current class list
- [ ] Copies of course outline
- [ ] Name cards for students to fill out and bring to future classes if students don't already have permanent nameplates as part of the program
- [ ] Water or juice for yourself

TABLE 4-3 Sample Student Information Card

Student Background Information
MGMT 1000: Fundamentals in Business

Name: E-mail:

Address: Phone number:

Previous Educational Experience: (list most recent first)

Previous Work Experience: (list position, company, major responsibilities)

Current or Intended Major/Concentration:

Career Aspirations/Goals:

5

CHAPTER FIVE

Improving Your Teaching Using Student Feedback

Many schools have a comprehensive, formal student course evaluation process, usually completed at the end of the term. Although these evaluations may provide you useful insights into your teaching effectiveness, the feedback will be received too late to make adjustments during the existing term.

CHAPTER 5 at a Glance

Use informal feedback to adjust your teaching plan on the fly

- Monitor nonverbal cues to assess student interest and engagement
- Obtain verbal feedback by asking students for direct input

Take the time after each class to note how things went

- Highlight key points to incorporate into the next class
- Note thoughts and ideas for the next time you teach the course

Collect written feedback to make ongoing improvements to the course

- Determine what elements of the course you want to assess
- Obtain the input you need
- Develop a plan to act on the input
- Share and discuss your plan with the class

Leverage end-of-term evaluations to improve the next iteration of your course

- Conduct any evaluation processes required by your school
- Supplement with customized feedback to obtain more detail
- Synthesize findings to determine what to do differently next time

Therefore, it's important to supplement end-of-term evaluation with processes that allow you to make "real-time" adjustments during the term. Regular input from your students can give you valuable insights that will prevent small issues from snowballing, improve the overall learning environment in your classroom, and allow you to improve your teaching before end-of-term evaluations are conducted.

There are a number of different approaches for gathering feedback beyond the standardized, comprehensive end-of-term evaluations conducted by many schools. You can use either informal or formal feedback processes, depending on your rapport with the students, personal preference, and type of information sought. Feedback approaches may include observing the nonverbal cues of your students, collecting class-by-class feedback, open-ended feedback, midterm feedback, and supplemental end-of-term feedback. You'll find that all of these sources of feedback provide vital information for continuous improvement. Particularly when you first start teaching, using a variety of techniques will allow you to generate the feedback loops you need to ensure you are effective in the classroom.

Use Informal Feedback to Adjust Your Teaching Plan on the Fly

Informal feedback refers to any verbal or nonverbal method used to assess how each class is going. This is different from the formal feedback mechanisms conducted by the school at the end of the term. This type of feedback is easy to collect and does not require much effort. Moreover, you often obtain very useful input which can be acted upon immediately, while the class is still in progress.

Monitor nonverbal cues to assess student interest and engagement

One of the simplest methods for obtaining feedback during the class is to monitor nonverbal cues. For example, body language such as nodding heads, sitting forward, smiling, questioning faces, and arched eyebrows indicate active, interested students.

Conversely, sleepy eyes, side conversations, and distracted students probably indicate that you have to make some adjustments to regain your class's attention. If you conclude you are losing your students' interest, the first thing you should try to discover is whether your teaching is at fault or whether there are other explanations for their behavior (e.g., room too hot, student fatigue, mid-term week, flu season, or pub night).

If your teaching approach appears to be the cause, you have several choices. You can simply start modifying your approach or shifting to new content to see if interest picks up. For example, if you're paying attention to nonverbal cues and notice that everyone in the class looks lost, you can adjust your agenda to spend an extra few minutes on that segment, explaining the concept more fully. In some cases, the cause of student disinterest may be a result of your delivery mode. Try something new or more interactive to see if an improvement results. You might even try something completely different by having students engage in a quick, physical activity like stretching.

Obtain verbal feedback by asking students for direct input

Another option is to ask students for specific input and ideas for improving the class. It would be beneficial to state upfront that both positive and negative feedback are welcome and that both are critical for ensuring the best learning environment possible. Asking for feedback in class may give you the input needed to understand what is going well and what you might modify. For example, in gauging whether you are moving through content too rapidly or too slowly, questions such as "Is everyone with me?" or "Everybody ready to move on?" or "Are we moving too fast?" offer a quick feedback method. Or, if you want to determine whether the class wants to elaborate on an issue, a question such as, "Any questions, thoughts, or comments?" works well.

Alternatively, you may ask students for direct verbal feedback on how a particular segment of the class went. You may ask for input on the content covered or the delivery mode used. For instance, you might ask students whether the debate just used in class was a good means of discussing the pros and cons of labor unions. Or, in an accounting class, you might ask students for feedback on the specific topics you selected to discuss from the assigned textbook chapter.

You might feel that students would be reluctant to share such information in class, fearing grade repercussions for negative comments or chiding from their peers if they give positive feedback. If this is the case, you could wait until the break or the end of class to casually join in on some student conversations, or you could seek some one-on-one feedback from specific students on how things are going, what's working, what isn't working, and why. This builds positive student rapport, and the students will appreciate the opportunity to comment. You may also want to use anonymous written forms of feedback, which are discussed later in this chapter.

Take the Time after Each Class to Note How Things Went

While a class is still fresh in your mind, you will find it beneficial to take a little time at the end to note how things went. These notes might include your personal opinions of how particular segments of the course were received, students' thoughts and reactions about different class segments, and/or ideas that come into your mind about how to improve this class session for the next time. Jotting down thoughts about how things went and ideas for improvement will help ensure class-to-class continuity in the present term and will also provide a platform from which you can make improvements for the next time you teach the course.

Highlight key points to incorporate into the next class

After each class, take the time to write down any unfinished topics or issues you want to address in the next class. Remember to incorporate and address those issues when preparing for your next class. This will ensure that you appear organized and will also communicate that you care about the continuity of your students' learning.

Note thoughts and ideas for the next time you teach the course

When you are teaching a course for the first time, it is often difficult to predict how things will go. Therefore, after each class, it is useful to take a little time to reflect on both content and process elements of the class. This will make sure that the next time you teach the course, you will be able to make improvements based on what you've learned from this teaching experience.

For broad, overarching changes, you might want to note details on the course syllabus. For class-specific changes, use your class process map (see Chapter 2, *Getting Ready for Each Class*). You can note overall impressions of how specific cases or readings were received, how various delivery modes worked, or how the timing allocated to each topic fit the overall pace of the class. Finally, beyond just noting your impressions, use the insights you've gained to generate thoughts and ideas about what to do differently when you teach this class the next time.

Collect Written Feedback to Make Ongoing Improvements to the Course

The end of the term is too late to have any impact on the current course. Therefore, it is useful to collect written feedback at various points throughout the term. This written feedback allows you to tap more systematically into the perceptions of the entire class, to receive input on how the overall course is going at that point, and to make timely improvements.

To maximize the benefits of written feedback, determine the elements you want to assess, establish the method of obtaining feedback, and develop a plan for sharing and acting on the feedback. Committing to this process will not only improve your effectiveness in the classroom, but also will demonstrate your respect for your students' ideas and input.

Determine what elements of the course you want to assess

You can choose to collect written feedback about any number of dimensions of the course. As well, you can choose to seek more general, broad-brushed reactions to the course or a class, or you can focus on the specifics of content, delivery, or evaluation methods within a class.

Obtain the input you need

The One-Minute Memo is one of the simplest and easiest tools for obtaining student feedback during the term. All that is involved is asking students to take a few minutes to anonymously write down answers to a handful of simple questions.

For example, broad-brushed feedback can be obtained by asking questions such as, "What is going well in this course?" or "What are your suggestions for improvement?"

More specific feedback questions on content might include asking students, "What part of the class was most valuable to you? Why?" or "What part of the class was most unclear to you? Why?" Class delivery feedback questions might ask students questions such as "How did you find the pace of today's class?" or "Should we incorporate more group work into the course?" or a more open-ended question such as "What tips do you have for conducting class discussions in future?"

One-Minute Memos can be used once around the midterm week or several times throughout the term. Excellent opportunities to conduct One-Minute Memos are after tests, assignments, or when your class just isn't going as well as you'd planned. See Table 5-1 for a **Sample One-Minute Memo**.

As an alternative to conducting a One-Minute Memo in class, you may be able to collect written feedback online, particularly if your school has an online end-of-term evaluation process already in place.

In addition, there are several other approaches you might use to collect input from your students on how the course is going. For instance, if you'd like to collect feedback after every class, you might use a variation of the One-Minute Memo where you ask specifically what the students thought about the content or process of a particular class. See Table 5-2 for a **Sample Class-by-Class Feedback Questionnaire**.

Finally, you may want to administer an open-ended questionnaire. This approach is particularly beneficial for gaining rich insight from students into specific aspects of the course such as pace, content, or relevance of readings. See Table 5-3 for a **Sample Open-Ended Questionnaire**.

Develop a plan to act on the input

After collecting feedback using the One-Minute Memo, look for patterns and consistent themes, both positive and negative, across your students' responses. Next, organize those themes and patterns into actionable categories. For example, if you asked the question, "What is going well in the course"?, you may get feedback that can be clustered around the topics of course content, classroom dynamics, and course delivery. Once you have the key themes identified, categorize student comments into those that are positive and those that are negative around that theme. See Table 5-4, **One-Minute Memo: Analysis**

and Action, for an example of how to analyze One-Minute Memo feedback. Table 5-5, **One-Minute Memo: Analysis and Action Worksheet**, offers a blank analysis worksheet.

Remember that these memos create an opportunity to elicit positive feedback as well as negative, so be sure to take the positive comments to heart as much as the negative ones. The important point is not to take negative comments personally, but rather to extract what is relevant and useful for improving both the course and your teaching style. For example, suppose you received a comment about being too young to be an instructor in a course. Though you might consider ways to convey your experience or increase your professionalism, this is really not a comment you can do anything about—you are the age that you are! With this in mind, try not to let a comment like this one impact your performance. Hard as it might be, chalk it up to strengthening character and move on.

Another important consideration as you develop action steps is to try not to alienate those students who are happy with how things are going. With this in mind, always ensure you've checked to see what students indicated was going well before making dramatic changes. Moreover, as you're sharing the action steps you're considering, you may want to get a quick read from the class about whether everyone is in agreement with the changes you plan to make. For example, maybe a handful of students in a strategy course suggested that you incorporate more group work into the second half of the semester. Before making dramatic changes, you may want to check with the entire class to ensure that the sentiment is shared.

Share and discuss your plan with the class

After you have collected feedback from your students, be sure to spend a few minutes responding to the feedback in the next class. It is important that the students understand how you are using their input. For example, you might say, "It was great to hear that many of you thought that X, Y, and Z were going well." "Suggestions that came up included 1, 2, and 3. So we'll be making changes such as the following in the next few weeks of the course." Even if these changes don't end up going as well as you'd expected, the students will give you credit for having listened to and acted upon their input.

Leverage End-of-Term Evaluations to Improve the Next Iteration of Your Course

A vital element of continuous improvement of your course is end-of-term feedback. This feedback gives the students an opportunity to step back from the course and provide an overall assessment, as well as give ideas for improvement that can be incorporated into future offerings of the course.

Conduct any evaluation processes required by your school

Most likely, your school has a standardized student evaluation process that is conducted at the end of the term. You should understand how this evaluation is conducted and any institutional norms in collecting this end-of-term feedback. For example, some schools have online end-of-term evaluations and others use paper. Or, in some schools, end-of-term feedback is administered by someone other than the instructor.

You should also try early in the term to obtain a copy of the form used so that you are familiar with the dimensions students will be using for their evaluations. Finding out when and how this evaluation is conducted is also useful for ensuring you've allocated sufficient time in your class planning to conduct the evaluation if it is done in class.

The nature and type of information provided to faculty based on their end-of-term course evaluations also vary by school. Some schools may only provide the original course evaluation forms back to faculty. Other schools may give instructors a detailed analysis of trends and patterns in their course evaluations. In addition, the turnaround time for return of course evaluations differs by school.

Supplement with customized feedback to obtain more detail

You might also want to supplement the required end-of-term evaluations with a qualitative questionnaire focused on obtaining more detailed feedback on specific aspects of your course. A customized feedback form allows you to obtain concrete ideas for refining and improving the course for subsequent terms.

Areas that you might want to cover on this customized form include: feedback on overall course content, relative assessments of each class in the course, suggestions for delivery, and thoughts about the evaluation vehicles used.

See Table 5-6 for a **Sample Supplemental End-of-Term Feedback** form. To capture optimal student feedback, we recommend you attach a summary of the course topics and activities on a class-by-class basis. Table 5-7 provides an illustrative **List of Topics and Activities for Supplemental End-of-Term Feedback**.

Synthesize findings to determine what to do differently next time

Upon receiving the feedback from both the required evaluations and your customized supplement, it is extremely valuable to take an hour or so to digest the comments and reflect. Read through all the feedback collected, synthesize your findings, and briefly sketch out ideas for improving the course for the next time you teach it.

By the time you reach the end of the term, you may be tempted to shelve student comments. However, it is almost impossible to interpret comments three to six months after the course is completed. Therefore, it's important to take the time to revisit the course while it is still fresh in your mind. Your most creative ideas for improving the course likely will surface upon receipt of the feedback. In addition, responding proactively to student feedback by making changes in your course reinforces the integrity of the end-of-term evaluation process.

FREQUENTLY ASKED QUESTIONS

Is it really necessary to discuss the feedback with the students?

Yes. If you're not prepared to communicate and take action based on the feedback, don't ask for it. Instructors gain significant credibility when they demonstrate to students that they are genuinely listening to, and taking action on, their comments. So after collecting any type of feedback, communicate what you've learned, what actions you plan to take, and ensure that you follow through on what you've committed to do.

How should I react if the student feedback is really "ugly" and very negative?

Listen to and learn from negative feedback, but don't let it debilitate you. Those negative comments can take the wind out of your sails. The key is to recognize that you can't please everyone. But a consistent pattern of negative feedback about a particular aspect of your teaching probably does indicate that this is an area you need to work on. As mentioned earlier in the chapter, try not to take negative feedback personally.

It is also useful to remember that many students are inexperienced in giving formal feedback. You can role model effective feedback through your grading practices by making sure you are constructive in your feedback and highlighting both strong and weak elements of the student submissions. You might find that students adopt this same kind of style when giving you feedback.

What should I do if the students suggest dropping a particular topic or class in their feedback?

Start by probing whether the feedback suggests the topic is not worth discussing in class or whether students are suggesting it should be dropped from the course. In the case of the former, whether you agree or disagree with their comments, you can incorporate this information into next year's teaching plan.

If the students are suggesting that the topic should be dropped from the course, then make your own determination as to whether you agree with that opinion. Students offer a unique and powerful perspective on the value of your course content. So, if a majority of students suggest a topic should be dropped, it is worthwhile to consider their advice carefully.

If you agree that a topic should be dropped from the course, your discretion in this regard may be limited by whether the course is core or elective. If it's a core course, you might try sharing the feedback with the course director to elicit discussion. If it's an elective, you'll likely have more degrees of freedom to take action.

On the other hand, while it's important to be responsive to feedback, you need to trust your instincts about the value of certain approaches or content. Sometimes students may suggest dropping a topic because it was ineffectively taught and they have missed its anticipated value. In these cases, sticking with the topic but revisiting your approach is a good idea.

Finally, keep in mind that just because a particular class evokes a strong opinion doesn't mean it hasn't been a great learning opportunity for students. For example, a class on a topic such as diversity, gender, ethics, or social responsibility often will elicit strong reactions—both positive and negative. Indeed, some of these classes are the ones that students will e-mail you about years later and say, "Although I disliked that one class at the time, I real-

ize now how important it was." In short, the bottom line is that you should listen to the students' feedback, but also rely on your own assessment of what content is critical.

If students continually miss class, are they sending a message?

Often, a strong nonverbal cue about your performance is high absenteeism rates over an extended period. A large number of students missing just one class might be explained by many external circumstances, such as mid-terms or flu season. If external circumstances are not the reason, you may want to pull aside some of the students who are attending to find out what's wrong.

Are there other methods of collecting feedback on my teaching rather than asking students?

There are several other methods for gaining insight into your teaching. For example, you might invite a more experienced colleague into your class and ask her to share her reactions and suggestions. If your school has a teaching support office, they may have "expert" teachers who will volunteer to observe teachers in their classrooms and give feedback. You might also consider having one of your class sessions videotaped or inviting a Ph.D student to attend your class and share her thoughts.

TABLE 5-1 Sample One-Minute Memo

FUNDAMENTAL BUSINESS PRINCIPLES – MGMT 1020
Course Feedback
October 10, 2XXX

Now that we've had a few classes together I want to gather some feedback about your perceptions of this course. I'd like to understand what aspects of this course are working well and also which areas need to be improved. Essentially, my goal is to ensure that you're getting the most value from this course.

Keep in mind that this is completely voluntary and anonymous. I will be the only person reading these evaluations, and your answers will in no way impact your grades. Do not put your name on this paper. Please be honest and feel free to add any other comments at the bottom.

What is going well with this course? (Topics, content, delivery modes, teaching style, evaluation, etc.)

What ideas do you have for improvement? Be bold, creative, and as explicit as possible.

Other Comments

Thank you very much for your feedback. I'll be summarizing your comments and sharing them with you in the next class.

TABLE 5-2 Sample Class-by-Class Feedback Questionnaire*

CLASS FEEDBACK – MGMT 2000

Class Title: ______________________________

1. One key takeaway from today's class is:

2. Best part of today's class or biggest "aha"!:

3. Weakest part of class to improve or omit:

4. Other thoughts about today's class:

*Thanks to Steve Weiss for sharing his template for class-by-class feedback.

TABLE 5-3 Sample Open-Ended Questionnaire*

MIDTERM FEEDBACK – MGMT 2000

Please take a few minutes to give me some feedback on this course to help me better plan our remaining classes. Do not hesitate to be critical; and please offer suggestions that you feel might improve the course.

1. Have you found the course to be well organized?

2. Are you finding the course interesting? Is it meeting your learning objectives?

3. Have you found the readings valuable? Are you doing the readings regularly? Do you find that the readings provide good background and preparation for class discussion?

4. Are the written assignments helpful?

5. Do you feel you have adequate opportunity to contribute to class discussion?

6. What ideas for improvement do you have?

7. Other comments?

*Thanks to Joyce Zemans for sharing her template for class-by-class feedback.

TABLE 5-4 One-Minute Memo: Analysis and Action

If you take the time to collect feedback, it is important to communicate with the students what actions you will take as a result. A useful method for both analyzing qualitative feedback and sharing the results of that analysis with your class is a content-analysis table, such as the one below.

As you can see, there are three columns. In the first column—"What's Going Well"—you would extract positive comments about the course, organized around meaningful sub-headings such as Classroom Dynamics, Content Relevance, and Design and Layout of the Course. In the second column—"Ideas for Improvement"—you would extract negative comments about the course, organized around the same meaningful sub-headings. In the final column—"Action Steps"—you would outline the actions you intend to take as a result of both the positive and negative feedback provided.

	WHAT'S GOING WELL?	IDEAS FOR IMPROVEMENT?	ACTION STEPS
Classroom Dynamics	■ Clear, crisp presentation ■ Class discussions encouraged and facilitated well ■ Dynamic and warm environment	■ Case discussions seem to follow the same format every week	■ Inject debate, role plays, class splits, breakouts, pertinent movie clips into case discussions
Content Relevance			
Design and Layout of the Course			
Prof's Style			
Projects			
Other			

TABLE 5-5 One-Minute Memo: Analysis and Action Worksheet

	WHAT'S GOING WELL?	IDEAS FOR IMPROVEMENT?	ACTION STEPS
Prof's Style			
Evaluation			
Design and Layout of the Course			
Delivery Modes			

TABLE 5-6 Sample Supplemental End-of-Term Feedback

FUNDAMENTALS IN INTERNATIONAL BUSINESS
MGMT 6400 - FALL 2XXX

Listed on the attached sheet are the topics and cases we covered this semester. In order to keep improving the course, it would be helpful if you could provide feedback.

1. Please list which 5 topics/cases were your "most favorite" and why.

Most Favorite: **Comments about Case or Topic**

1.______________________________

2.______________________________

3.______________________________

4.______________________________

5.______________________________

If you felt the topic was important but that the case could be improved, or that the case was good but the topic less valuable, please note that as well.

2. Please list 5 topics/cases which were your "least favorite" and why.

Least Favorite: **Comments about Case or Topic**

1.______________________________

2.______________________________

3.______________________________

4.______________________________

5.______________________________

3. How did you feel about cases, lectures, DVDs, and small groups as learning approaches in this course?

4. How did you feel about the team projects? (e.g., having your choice of what organization to explore? Being able to self-select into teams? Having team presentations?)

5. What did you think of the guest speakers in this course?

6. Are there other ideas you have for making this course better?

THANK YOU VERY MUCH FOR YOUR INPUT!

TABLE 5-7 List of Topics and Activities for Supplemental End-of-Term Feedback

FUNDAMENTALS OF INTERNATIONAL MANAGEMENT
MGMT 6400 - FALL 2XXX

#	Class Topic	Case/Videos
I. Introduction and Overarching Frameworks		
Class 1:	Overview of the Course, Getting Warmed up, Frameworks	Smith Corp.
II. Managing in Today's Global Environment		
Class 2:	The Global Economy and Marketplace	Jones Corp DVD: Issues in Multinational Corporations
Class 3:	Changing Global Technology	Edge Software Ltd.
Class 4:	Managing Cross-Cultural Complexities	Cross-Cultural Simulation
III. History of Modern Management		
Class 5:	Early Thinkers	Biography of F. Taylor
Class 6:	Challenges to the Early Thinkers	Debate
Class 7:	Breaking the Paradigms	Runway Airlines Inc.
Class 8:	Recent Innovations in International Management	Guest Speaker
Class 9:	Team Projects	Student Presentations
IV. ...		

6

CHAPTER SIX

Grading

The focus of our teaching should be on learning rather than grading. In a successful class, students will realize all the learning objectives for the course and be able to take their knowledge forward into their next business course or their job in the business world. Grading is, however, the indicator used by the students, faculty, and prospective employers to measure learning and is, therefore, of significant interest and concern to business students.

For many instructors, grading can be one of the most stressful, challenging, and time-consuming parts of teaching. However, it is an essential element of the learning

CHAPTER 6 at a Glance

Prepare to grade

- Know your school's processes and norms for grading
- Allot sufficient time in your schedule for grading
- Develop your grading key and criteria
- Develop your grading spreadsheet
- Determine how you will provide comments

Evaluate the submissions

- Get an overall impression of class performance
- Provide specific comments and suggestions inside the document
- Offer summary comments on the front page
- Check for fairness and consistency

Explain your grading process to your class

- Provide feedback on overall class performance
- Communicate grading key and criteria
- Explain how you will handle grading concerns
- Invite students to meet with you for more discussion

Handle difficult grading discussions effectively

- Diffuse the situation with a "cool-off" period
- Prepare in advance for any conversations about grades
- Focus on learning rather than "the grade"

Stay on top of the administrative aspects of grading

- Maintain accurate, up-to-date records
- Keep students informed about how they are doing

experience for students and, therefore, an important part of our job. Since students take our feedback very seriously, a systematic process for grading is essential to ensure that grading is fair, equitable, and constructive. A systematic process for grading also ensures efficiency, which saves us time in the long run. Although your grading task will vary to some extent depending on the evaluation instrument you have selected (See Table 1-3, **Common Student Evaluation Methods** in Chapter 1, *Pulling Your Course Together*), there are some general principles that are important to all grading endeavors.

Start by spending some time preparing to grade. This may include getting to know your school's norms and guidelines, creating a grading key and criteria, and developing your grading spreadsheet. As you embark on the actual grading of your students' submissions, take the time to scan through the papers first to gain an overall sense of class performance. As you mark each submission, ensure that feedback is detailed and consistent. When handing back the papers, it is important to discuss key patterns and performance across the class as well as to describe your grading process in detail.

More than likely you'll have to deal with a few students who are disappointed with their evaluation. Ensure that you have steps in place to deal with these occurrences so you can ensure these interactions are productive rather than frustrating or excessively emotional. Finally, keeping up-to-date records and constantly providing students with feedback on their performance are additional components of the grading process.

Prepare to Grade

Prior to grading, there are a few essential steps that you can take to ensure grading effectiveness. First, it is important that you have a good sense of the grading guidelines and norms at your institution. You need to understand what grade is considered a pass/fail, how grades are normally articulated, and if there are any guidelines in terms of grade distribution. This will help you avoid violating institutional norms and practices that the students have come to expect.

Second, grading always takes more time than anticipated, so be sure to allocate enough time for this key aspect of the student learning process. Plan for some "grader fatigue" and be realistic about how many papers you can grade in one sitting. You may find it helpful to spread out your grading task in short time periods and possibly over a number of days, depending on how many papers you have to grade.

Third, have a good understanding of the learning you expect to be demonstrated and some predetermined criteria by which you will evaluate students' performance. Develop a grading key to justify the grade you allocate to each portion of the paper or exam. Finally, create a spreadsheet for easy recording and calculation of the grades and have a system for communicating grades to your students throughout the term.

Know your school's processes and norms for grading

A critical step in preparing to grade for the first time is to ensure that you are familiar with the policies, guidelines, and norms for grading that apply at your school and within your specific department. You should also determine whether grading is done on a curve, with grades allocated according to fixed distribution standards. This might mean that fewer than 10% of the students can receive an "A" and 30% of the class should receive a B-. If grades are curved, also determine what a typical grading distribution looks like in courses similar to the one you're teaching.

Alternatively, you might find that grades are not subject to any curves and can be determined solely by the instructor. If that's the case for the course you're teaching, you should ensure that you've reviewed university-specific handbooks for grading guidelines, as well as discussed grading plans with the area coordinator or course director so you can be sure that you're following your school's norms.

Even without grade distribution norms, you should anticipate a normal distribution for your class grades and avoid the temptation to give all students good grades.

Other pertinent details about grading that you may want to ascertain include:

- Whether grades are given as letters or numbers
- How grades are posted
- Whether grading is done blind (where the grader does not know whose paper he is grading)
- The grading appeal process
- How grades are submitted
- The required turnaround time for end-of-term grades
- Re-marking policies

Allocate sufficient time in your schedule for grading

Make sure that you allocate sufficient time in your schedule so that you can grade your students' submissions fairly and provide constructive feedback. Grading can be a very arduous process, and you'll likely need to allocate much more time than you initially anticipate. Experienced instructors know that creating the grading key, providing detailed comments, and recording grades take time. In addition, to ensure consistency and fairness in grading, you'll need to punctuate this grading process with breaks. You'll likely find that you can't grade for more than a few hours at a time and remain mentally alert.

Although you may be tempted to promise students that their submissions will be returned in the next class, you may soon realize that such a promise is difficult to keep. Be realistic with students about your turnaround time. Students tend to be anxious about their grades and to be impatient about waiting for their results. It is important to set a realistic expectation on turnaround time and deliver on your commitment in order to minimize disappointment. Student feedback is critical for learning, so submissions should be returned to students with ample time to learn from your comments and to understand your grading style prior to the next evaluation component.

A good way to get a rough estimate of how long it will take you to complete the entire grading process is to use the first few submissions as a benchmark. Then multiply that time period by the remaining number of submissions. Depending on the nature of the student submission, you should add up to another 6 hours to take into consideration the preparation time discussed earlier in the chapter along with checking for fairness and consistency and writing summary comments and other grading details.

Develop your grading key and criteria

Before you start grading, do the exam or assignment yourself so you are clear about your expectations and what you are looking for in the student submissions. Ensure your evaluation approach reinforces the learning objectives and goals for the course, and determine if there is one correct answer or several equally viable solutions.

If you are looking for a single, correct answer, as might be the case in a finance or economics assignment, decide if you will give partial marks and how that will be determined. You need to decide how you will recognize student effort that demonstrates partial understanding of the material, yet is unable to produce the correct answer.

If you are using multiple-choice or true-or-false questions, determine if you will penalize wrong answers to discourage guessing (if you do intend to penalize wrong answers, be sure to communicate that to the students before they write the test).

For other grading situations, such as a strategy or marketing case analysis, there may be many acceptable answers. Your preparation will help you clarify the criteria that you will use in evaluating responses. With these types of submissions, you might reward clear logic and flow or financial justification.

To prepare for grading, construct an answer key or guide which delineates the correct answer or the standards and criteria that will be used to evaluate and assess the various components of each student's submission. See Table 6-1 for a **Sample Grading Key for an Essay Question**.

In addition to developing clear criteria for grading, it is important to establish the relative weighting of different elements of the exam, assignment, or project. You should break down a grade into various subcomponents and elements, and assign weighting or points to these various elements. This is more effective than simply giving an overall grade to the assignment. For example, when grading a case submission, you may allocate a percentage of the total grade to each of: diagnosis, analysis, assessment of alternatives, recommendations, and implementation plan.

Develop your grading spreadsheet

Before starting the grading process, ensure that you have a blank spreadsheet for recording grades. It should include columns for the students' names, their student number, a column for every component that students will be graded on during the term, as well as summary columns for tallying final grades. See Table 6-2 for a **Sample Grading Template**.

If you keep this spreadsheet up-to-date throughout the term, you will find communication with the students and calculation of midterm and final grades a simpler task. See Table 6-3 for a completed **Sample Grading Spreadsheet**.

Determine how you will provide comments

To provide sufficient opportunity for learning, you need to provide grading feedback that tells a student more than simply whether she was right or wrong. Typically, additional comments customized to the student submission are required, and you need to consider the format you plan to use for writing comments.

In smaller classes, instructors may be able to provide extensive comments within the document itself. In larger classes, it may be helpful to use a comment key whereby numbers are used to denote generic comments that are detailed on a summary sheet. For instance, in an essay question for an organizational behavior course, a frequent error of many students may be that they failed to discuss the opposing view of a particular argument. Therefore, rather than writing this comment for every student, number 6 might state, "Outlining alternative viewpoints in detail would have strengthened this answer." You may also want to use a numbering system to provide specific comments. This is best when instructors need more room to explain their comment or when an instructor's writing is illegible.

Your grading process also may differ depending on the type of evaluation component. For example, for cases, projects, and papers, you may want to provide summary feedback on the first page of the document in addition to the more detailed comments within the document. See Table 6-4, **Sample Summary Comments** for a sample feedback form.

Preparing feedback forms electronically is another efficient approach if you are handy with a computer and find keyboarding faster than writing comments. Prepare an outline of the key grading points with room for comments. Once typed, the comment sheets can be printed or e-mailed for distribution to students, as well as stored for future reference. Repeat comments are quickly handled by using the copy and paste functions, and modifications to your feedback and grades are easily accommodated as you work through the assignments. Once you have finished the assignments, you can quickly stack the comment forms and look for consistency in your grading.

Evaluate the Submissions

When you actually move to grading, it is a good idea to start off by conducting a quick scan of all your students' submissions. With an overall impression of how your class has done, you're ready to begin evaluating each submission in detail. As you grade each student's work, keep in mind that students tend to focus quickly on the grade and then look to see what you had to say specifically about their submission. A grade should be supported with both specific comments within the body of the document and some summary feedback on the front page.

Most instructors provide detailed comments within the document as they read it and then step back and reflect on the entire document to develop their summary comments.

Both detailed and summary comments should address what was done well and offer suggestions about how the submission might have been improved. Thoughtful comments give students the feedback they need to understand the rationale for their grade. They also contribute to students' learning cycles and enable them to gain insight into how they can perform more effectively in future assignments, exams, and projects.

Finally, once the feedback and grade decision is complete, take the time to ensure consistency across all submissions and make modifications as required.

Get an overall impression of class performance

Although you might be tempted to dive right into the first submission by reading it thoroughly and writing comments, we recommend that you try first to get an overall sense of the class performance. This will ensure that you don't start grading your papers only to realize later that the comments you've written need to be altered or that the first set of papers' grades are skewed. You can avoid these inefficiencies and inconsistencies in marking by first getting an overall impression of class performance.

Start out by quickly scanning the papers, exams, or assignments (or at least a random sampling) to identify the approach various students have taken. Doing a quick scan gives you an idea of the range of answers that you'll be grading so you get a sense of the standard to apply and how to distinguish an excellent submission from an average or below-average submission. Without conducting a quick scan, you run the risk of basing your grade distribution on a non-representative sample of the class. For example, you might give "C"s to the first five papers you read, only to realize that the rest of the papers are even weaker than the first five! In this case, those "C"s you assigned could end up being some of the best papers in the class.

Scanning the stack also gives you the benefit of having in advance a rough sense of the range of student abilities so you know how best to approach grading each student's submission. You might find that reading a student's submission from beginning to end makes the most sense. Alternatively, after your initial scan, you may decide that grading each question across all student submissions before continuing to the next question is the best approach. This likely will depend on whether the entire submission is an integrated unit or each question is distinct and self-contained. For example, when grading a case, you might want to read the student papers in their entirety so that you're able to assess whether problems they've identified are covered in their recommendations and whether their analysis is integrated. In contrast, for a finance course, you'll likely want to grade one problem across the whole class before moving to the second problem.

Provide specific comments and suggestions inside the document

Either you or your grader will read and evaluate each submission thoroughly and provide comments to students. While you're reading the submissions, we suggest that you note comments in the margins on specific aspects of the submission while the detail is fresh in your mind. You might consider writing comments in pencil so you have some flexibility to change your comments as you complete your grading.

This feedback should provide students with input on their key points, arguments, and logic. Highlight strengths, inconsistencies, and incomplete analysis. Provide comments that are constructive and specific to ensure that your students clearly understand your feedback. For example, rather than simply writing, "This analysis needs to be strengthened," offer a comment such as, "This analysis could be strengthened by providing further financial justification using a balance sheet or income statement." If a numerical calculation is incorrect, show the correct answer so that the student can learn from his mistake.

Offer summary comments on the front page

Once you've completed your detailed comments, provide overview comments on the front page to give students overall feedback on their work. When developing these summary comments, look for themes and patterns throughout the document that capture the student's overall performance. For instance, if a student consistently demonstrates a detailed analysis across many components of the paper, commending this strength on the front page is a good idea.

Rather than writing initial thoughts about summary feedback directly on the document, you may want to use post-it notes to jot down some of these key ideas or to capture them in your electronic feedback form on your computer. You may also find these post-it notes or electronic documents useful for assigning tentative grades. They enable you to do a "rough draft" of the grades and summary comments that you can finalize *after* you have done a final check for consistency and fairness.

When writing your final draft of summary comments, offer frank but constructive feedback. For example, start with some positive comments on what was done well and then some overall comments on what needs improvement. Working back from "what would it take to make this an 'A+' paper" might be a good frame of reference for you to keep in mind as you write these comments. These summary comments should provide a justification and rationale for the overall grade. See Table 6-4 again for **Sample Summary Comments**.

Check for fairness and consistency

As you progress towards finalizing your grades and comments, you should ensure that your grades are both fair and consistent. If the majority (or all) students incorrectly answer a particular question on a test or exam, perhaps the question was worded in a confusing way. Alternatively, you may have identified a key concept that requires additional teaching in the classroom. If your class grades deviate significantly from a normal distribution, reflect on why that might be the case. If your grades are clustered or skewed, be sure you have set appropriate performance standards and points of differentiation and have not fallen into the trap of trying to please everyone and giving all the students a "B."

Talk with colleagues to ensure that your grade distributions are aligned with the distributions of similar courses in your department. Also consider student motivation and morale. Students generally place a high value on the grades they achieve, and consistently low grades can be demoralizing and demotivating.

On the other hand, undeserved high grades can create a false sense of confidence or a lack of respect for the course. Refer back to the objectives you set out at the beginning of the term as you assess both the overall course distribution and your evaluation of individual students. Make sure your expectations are reasonable and that the students are learning what they need to know.

To ensure consistency, compare papers that have been assigned similar grades. The summary comments across the same grades should be similar in the balance of strengths and weaknesses. For instance, all "B+" work should share certain common elements, while all "B-" work should share a different set of common elements. In short, you should be able to clearly justify assigning one grade versus another. As a new instructor, in particular, you may find that you need to adjust some of your summary comments or even adjust a grade as you work through each pile. Here's where the benefit of doing a rough draft of the grades and comments on a post-it note or electronic document first will pay off.

Explain Your Grading Process to Your Class

An important step in the evaluation process is to discuss the grades with the students prior to handing them back. Although there is an abundance of feedback in the document itself, students are eager to hear general comments about the performance of the class, grade distribution, and the process by which you determined their individual grades. In addition, provide students with details about how grading concerns will be addressed. Stress the fact that the purpose of evaluation is to enhance their learning processes and that this submission is only one of several evaluation components, providing them with ample opportunity to recoup. Finally, it is important that you provide students with detail on how they can further discuss their submission with you if they so desire.

Provide some feedback about overall class performance

Business students often are very competitive and measure their performance relative not only to their own expectations, but also to the performance of their classmates. They often want to know how they have performed relative to their peers.

Before you return the graded assignments, provide some feedback about overall class performance. For example, you might want to highlight what was generally done well, common weaknesses, the mark distribution, the class average, and the grade range—highest and lowest grades. See Table 6-5, **Example of Overall Class Summary**.

Communicate grading key and criteria

As part of your in-class discussion of grades, you should communicate the grading key and criteria. This information will be useful for students as they read the comments on their papers. It is beneficial to have this discussion before handing back the graded assignments because once they have received their assignments they will be focused on their grade and may not hear much of what you are saying.

Explain how you will handle grading concerns

Not all students who receive a poor grade will be surprised or upset. Some recognize that they were not fully prepared for the test or that they rushed to complete an assignment. However, a few students may be very disappointed in their performance, feel they were fully prepared for the test or assignment, and may worry that they do not know how to be successful in your class. Other students may simply disagree with the grade you assigned and, in an effort to maximize their grades, may challenge your grading methodology.

Set the appropriate expectation about how you will handle grading concerns. Our recommendation is to adopt a policy of open dialogue about grading results and learning outcomes, but not to change grades except for significant, obvious grader errors, such as an error in the addition of subtotals. If you have been thorough in your grading process, provided a substantial number of comments to your students, and discussed your grading process in class, you can be confident in your stance that you don't revisit grades.

Invite students to meet with you for more discussion

Recognize that for some students, your comments and feedback may not provide enough information. Avoid addressing specific grade concerns in front of the whole class. Instead, invite students to come and see you for more discussion, but emphasize that you will focus on learning from the experience rather than negotiating the actual grade assigned.

An invitation to come and see you for more discussion gives you the opportunity to capture any outstanding student concerns. If you get a lot of students coming to see you, this might indicate that either your grading process or communication approach needs to be refined.

Handle Difficult Grading Discussions Effectively

Some students view their grades as a key measure of their performance and focus on strong grades to assist them in securing a job or scholarship. These students can have difficulty seeing their performance objectively. Although these students are in the minority, it is not uncommon to have a handful of students who are either upset or angry about their grade. You should consider the following tips for effectively handling difficult grading discussions.

Diffuse the situation with a cool-off period

Create a buffer between the time students receive their grades and the time you meet with them to discuss their grades. It is highly recommended that you avoid setting up discussion meetings immediately after class or even during the break of the class in which you hand back grades. First, students are often emotional about their grades, particularly when they first receive them. Second, if you meet with a student in class, be aware that your discussion might become a public display, particularly if the conversation becomes intense.

Instead, tell your students that if they have any questions about their grade, they can meet with you during your office hours or make an appointment. This "cool-off period" helps diffuse their immediate reactions and facilitates a more productive meeting. At the same time, try to meet any students with concerns before the next class so that issues can be resolved in a timely manner.

You may consider asking students for a written explanation of their question or concern and to return the paper with their request. This gives you time to organize your thoughts and also determine if a face-to-face meeting is required or a simple, written point of clarification will meet the needs of the student.

Consider defining a window in which you will entertain grade discussions, such as within one week of the assignment or test being returned.

For any meetings that you set up, restrict the time to less than 30 minutes in order to ensure that the meeting is focused, productive, and doesn't deteriorate into a battleground.

Prepare in advance for any conversations with students about grades

If you have access to a copy of the student's submission, start by reviewing it in advance. If you don't have access to a copy, ask the student if you can make a copy to refresh your memory about her performance. Next, check into the student's previous performance in the course to contextualize the grade she's received on this aspect of the course. Then, ensure that you have all the relevant materials on hand that you might want to refer to throughout your conversation with the student. Some reference materials that might be useful include: the grading criteria, the grade distribution, the class average, and your answer key, if applicable.

Finally, map out the approach you want to take in the meeting with the student and what points you want to highlight. For instance, you may want to prepare some additional comments to augment what you originally wrote on the student's paper. By preparing in advance, you will be equipped to handle grading discussions in an organized and well-informed manner, which conveys to students that your grading is fair and systematic.

Focus on learning rather than "the grade"

In every grading discussion, you want to ensure that students understand your reasons for assigning a grade. However, you don't want to engage in an extended discussion on grading, where you end up revisiting the same issues again and again, with no resolution in sight. Instead, try to direct the discussion towards what the student can learn from the experience and what he can take away to help improve her future performance. Again, keeping these discussions to less than 30 minutes helps ensure that the focus is on learning.

Stay on Top of the Administrative Aspects of Grading

Beyond effective grading of each element of the course, it is important that you establish a systematic process for managing the administrative side of grading. This includes both maintaining accurate records of students' performance and establishing a communication mechanism to keep students informed about how they are doing.

Maintain accurate, up-to-date records

Students may ask you for detailed information about their grades. Your school or department may require submission of all components of grades. Past students may call on you to provide references and recommendations for jobs they are seeking. All of these scenarios demand that you maintain an accurate and complete record of your students' performance and grades.

As mentioned earlier, one way of accomplishing this task is to prepare a spreadsheet prior to your first class that you can use to track all your students' grades throughout the term.

If class participation is a component of evaluation in your course, you should grade participation after each class. This might mean recording qualitative comments or some numeric "scores" right after each class. Ideally, as mentioned in Table 1-3, **Common Student Evaluation Methods** in Chapter 1, *Pulling Your Course Together*, you should be recording information on both the quality and quantity of each student's participation. Waiting until the end of the term to assign participation grades forces you to rely on your recollection of students' performance rather than on concrete data. Remember to keep these class participation records up-to-date so that you can share students' progress with them throughout the term.

Keep students informed about how they are doing

As mentioned throughout this chapter, students like to know how they are progressing in a course, so it is important to ensure your turnaround time for grading is fairly quick. If too much time elapses between handing in an assignment and receiving feedback, students likely will complain about the lag and also learn less from the feedback. A student submission that is returned a month later may no longer seem relevant because she likely will have moved on to focusing on new work and assignments. At the same time, you don't want to promise the return of assignments in too short a time period and not be able to deliver them.

In terms of communicating with your students, ensure you post grades in accordance with your school or department's norms (some schools post grades on glass bulletin boards while others e-mail student grades) and, again, do so in a timely fashion.

In courses where students receive grades for class participation, it is not only important to track performance, but also to allow students to access their participation grades on a regular basis. This will satisfy both students' curiosity about how they are doing and allow them to improve their participation in the class.

FREQUENTLY ASKED QUESTIONS

I've heard about "grading blind." What does it mean and how do you do it?

Grading blind means grading without knowing the identity of the student whose work you are evaluating. This technique is a good way to ensure that personal feelings about students do not bias your grading.

To make grading blind easier, have students put their name on a cover sheet you can flip over when grading, or ask them only to write their student ID number on their work rather than using their name. The number of digits in the students' ID numbers and the size of the class may influence whether you go with only ID numbers or prefer to have the name on a cover sheet that can be flipped over.

If you do blind grading, communicate this approach to your students so that they know their submissions will be evaluated objectively.

How can I best ensure consistency in grading?

Another aspect you may want to consider when developing your grading process is to plan for grading fatigue and other potential biases in your grading process. One approach that can minimize biases due to grading fatigue is to stack the papers according to grade and verify consistency between them.

A second tactic for developing your process is to ensure that the beginning of the pile is the same as the end of the pile. One way to address this is to start grading question one for student 1 ending with student 50, and then grade working backwards for question 2, starting with student 50 and ending with student 1.

I have a student in my office who disagrees with his grade. I've tried talking him through the grading process rationally, but we are still in disagreement. The student is persistent.

The first step may be to arrange another meeting with the student to discuss your grading decision. You may also want to probe a bit to find out the motive behind the student's behavior. For example, perhaps a student needs a particular GPA to obtain a scholarship, and he is counting on your course to bump up his average.

As a last resort, if you've already gone through the steps highlighted above—reviewed the submission, discussed your grading key, talked about overall class performance—you might suggest that the student file a grade appeal. Most schools have a grade appeal process for students who feel their grade is unfair. Typically the process involves other department members regrading the submission to determine whether your grade was fair.

How do I ensure that I am marking fairly?

All instructors bring with them a number of biases when grading that stem from past experiences and their personal perceptions of students. You should ensure that your grading process is as bias-free as possible. One tactic is to refer back to the objectives you set out both at the beginning of the term and for specific evaluation components when determining what deserves a particular grade. This information is communicated to students through the course syllabus and the evaluation handout. Fairness in grading is best achieved when you evaluate students on items for which they know they are responsible.

If you're not grading blind, keeping your evaluation process bias-free is going to be more difficult. You'll have to take extra precautions to ensure that students' performance, personality, and behavior beyond that particular evaluation component are not factors in your marking process. It's surprisingly easy—and often unconscious—for strong positive or negative feelings about a student to creep into your grading decisions.

Some of the suggestions offered above, such as verifying consistency across grade allocations and checking in with school norms and guidelines, also will help ensure fairness in your grading process.

Should I change my grading policies during the term if I'm getting many student complaints?

As a general rule, it is best to adhere to the policies you set out initially in your course outline. Changing your grading policies midstream can erode students' confidence and cause them to feel your grading system is not fair and consistent. For example, changing the content to be covered in exams, the weightings of evaluation components in a final grade, or the format of the exam inevitably leads to student frustration and loss of instructor credibility.

Nevertheless, grading can be challenging, particularly for new faculty members. Therefore, you might find yourself in the position of needing to modify your grading policy. For example, you may have administered a department-wide exam and realized too late that you haven't provided your students with some of the information they needed to perform well. Or, on your first round of grading, you may have graded either too harshly or too leniently. In cases such as these, the benefit of modifying your grading policies might outweigh the potential downside of continuing with your original plan. However, if you are considering making changes, check your department's policies. If changes are permitted, it is essential that you fully explain your rationale, provide sufficient justification to your students for the changes, and underscore the unusual nature of the situation.

What should I do if a student launches a formal grade appeal?

The student appeal process is different at every school. You should familiarize yourself with the process, which will be documented in the academic standards and policies. Usually, there are formal procedures and time frames in which a grade appeal can be initiated.

Typically, formal grade appeals are quite uncommon and can be avoided by open communication with the student about grading methodologies and a fair explanation of how the student's grade was calculated.

If an appeal is launched, you may be required to describe your grading methodology, and the student assignment in question may be re-evaluated by a colleague to validate the grade assigned by you.

You can check with a colleague or the program coordinator to understand more specifically how grade appeals are managed at your school.

How do I prevent students who have done poorly on an early assignment from disengaging from the course?

Students who have done poorly on an assignment or exam often may feel frustrated, angry, or upset. Their tendency may be to become demotivated and to disengage from the class. Therefore, you might want to go out of your way to reach out to those students. Highlight the fact that this assignment was only one of many evaluation components. You could also make an extra effort to get them involved in class discussions.

TABLE 6-1 Sample Grading Key for an Essay Question*

GRADING KEY
MIDTERM EXAM: MGMT 2000

QUESTION 1 Value: 20 points

POINTS	CONTENT OF ANSWER
0-5	The student demonstrates a poor understanding of the question and is unable to form a coherent, well-reasoned response. ■ Statements and opinions unsupported by factual evidence. ■ Little reference to course concepts. ■ May make references to current events, but needs to more clearly articulate their relevance or significance.
6-10	Offers a clearly stated thesis. Applies course concepts to a limited extent, but may not properly attribute sources. ■ Factual evidence may be sketchy but is relevant. ■ Quality of argument occasionally lacks consistency. ■ Statements may be contradictory or questionable in terms of their logic or likely efficacy.
11-15	Offers a clearly stated thesis. Appropriately draws upon and thoroughly applies relevant course concepts. ■ Makes a consistent, reasonable, and rational argument in support of position. ■ Successfully incorporates relevant factual evidence to bolster argument. ■ Clearly, comprehensively, and accurately relates question to relevant frameworks and models.
16-20	All of the content of an answer in the 11-15 mark range plus: ■ Incorporates additional models and frameworks discussed in lectures. ■ Acknowledges opposing opinions and viewpoints. ■ Identifies critical and competing perspectives and responds satisfactorily to them, resolving the intellectual gap. ■ Demonstrates logical, independent thinking on the subject beyond material learned from lectures, tutorials, and the textbook.

* Thanks to the TAs in the BBA Management 1000 Course at Schulich for sharing their grading key.

TABLE 6-2 Sample Grading Template

Course Number: ____________________
Course Name: ____________________
Grading Spreadsheet

LAST NAME	FIRST NAME	STUDENT NUMBER	MIDTERM EXAM (20%)	GROUP PAPER (20%)	CLASS PARTICIPATION (10%)	GROUP PRESENTATION (15%)	FINAL EXAM (35%)	OVERALL GRADE (%)	OVERALL GRADE (LETTER)

TABLE 6-3 Sample Grading Spreadsheet

MGMT 6900
FUNDAMENTALS OF BUSINESS
GRADING SPREADSHEET

LAST NAME	FIRST NAME	STUDENT NUMBER	MIDTERM EXAM (20%)	GROUP PAPER (20%)	CLASS PARTICIPATION (10%)	GROUP PRESENTATION (15%)	FINAL EXAM (35%)	OVERALL GRADE (%)	OVERALL GRADE (LETTER)
Student #1	Student #1	101010101	75	66	56	75	66	68%	C+
Student #2	Student #2	202020202	76	78	67	76	76	76%	B+
Student #3	Student #3	303030303	86	76	76	79	86	82%	A-
Student #4	Student #4	404040404	56	56	78	80	75	68%	C+
Student #5	Student #5	505050505	78	86	87	81	65	76%	C+
Student #6	Student #6	606060606	98	66	84	78	74	79%	B+
Student #7	Student #7	707070707	67	78	73	67	72	72%	B-
Student #8	Student #8	808080808	78	76	54	67	71	71%	B-
Student #9	Student #9	909090909	77	75	49	67	73	71%	B-
Student #10	Student #10	1010101010	74	77	91	66	78	77%	B+
Student #11	Student #11	1111111111	72	73	99	86	87	82%	A-
Student #12	Student #12	1212121212	86	71	76	78	76	77%	B+
Student #13	Student #13	1313131313	43	78	78	98	78	74%	B
Student #14	Student #14	1414141414	76	87	76	78	79	80%	A-
Student #15	Student #15	1515151515	78	81	78	76	79	79%	B+
Student #16	Student #16	1616161616	86	67	78	76	78	77%	B+
Student #17	Student #17	1717171717	88	55	79	78	91	80%	A-
Student #18	Student #18	1818181818	86	72	78	54	76	74%	B
Student #19	Student #19	1919191919	56	82	76	66	65	68%	C+
Student #20	Student #20	2020202020	77	91	74	78	66	76%	B
Student #21	Student #21	2121212121	89	99	66	89	54	76%	B
Student #22	Student #22	2222222222	78	76	69	76	59	70%	B-
Student #23	Student #23	2323232323	88	75	78	74	60	73%	B-
Student #24	Student #24	2424242424	80	78	66	72	76	76%	B

TABLE 6-4 Sample Summary Comments

TEAM PROJECT FEEDBACK - PROFESSOR DOE

Value: 40 points
Team Project Topic: Group A – Edge Software's War on Talent

Verbal Presentation: **Score: 7.5 out of 10**

- Well organized, well-delivered presentation
- Good diagnosis of success factors
- Clever examples
- Thoughtful bottom-line "takeaways"
- Additional background and history would have strengthened the presentation
- Some graphics were a bit difficult to read
- The presentation flow was choppy in spots

Written Report: **Score: 22 out of 30**
(Please see additional comments inside the report.)

- Interesting project
- Thoughtful analysis of advantages and disadvantages
- Insightful application
- Good reflections on lessons learned
- Diagnosis hit some of the key areas but could have been pushed further
- Structure of report was a bit hard to follow in certain places
- More in-depth data collection and research would have enhanced arguments
- Creative but unrealistic ideas on recommendations
- Pushing assessment a bit further would have strengthened report

Total Score: 29.5 out of 40
Letter Grade: B-

TABLE 6-5 Example of Overall Class Summary

EVALUATION OF GROUP PROJECTS

This project was worth 30 points and 30% of the final grade in this course, as stated on your syllabus and the Group Project handout.

Attached to your project is a Group Project Evaluation sheet, which offers summary comments, point allocations, a total point score, and a letter grade. Some additional comments are also provided in the text of the written document.

Breakdown and Components of Group Project (as stated on "Group Project" handout)

The breakdown of each section as stipulated on the Group Project handout is:

- **Verbal Presentation** - 10 points
- **Written Document** - 20 points

Introduction
- Executive summary
- Description of methods used in research
- Company background and history
- Motivating factors
- Current strategy

Analysis
- Elements of organizational design
- Implementation
- Effectiveness
- Advantages and disadvantages
- Recommendations for improvement
- Lessons learned

Each project receives a "Group Project Feedback" sheet, with summary comments, point allocations for the verbal presentation and written document, a total point score, and a letter grade. Additional comments are also provided in the text of the written document.

Grade, Percentage, and Point Conversions

To understand your numerical score and grade, see the table below for more information on points, 0 - 100% conversion, and grade conversion.

GRADE	POINTS	100% SCALE
A+	30	100
A+	29	96.7
A+	28	93.3
A	27	90.0
A	26	86.7
A-	25	83.3
A-	24	80.0
B+	23	76.7
B	22	73.3
B-	21	70.0
C+	20	66.7
C	19	63.3
C-	18	60.0
D+	17	56.7
D	16	53.3
D-	15	50.0

Class Performance

Overall, this was a great set of projects! Some were outstanding! The range of scores on these projects was from 70% (21) to 91% (27.5), and the average was 82% (24.6). Here is a distribution of the grades:

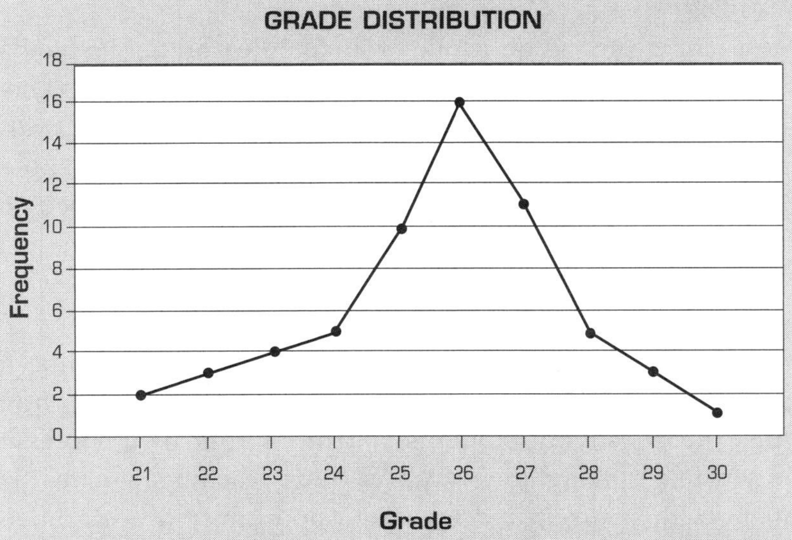

Other Thoughts

Finally, I am very open to discussing your projects with you. However, I do not change grades once my evaluation is complete, except for adjustments for addition errors.

Keep in mind, as noted above, that this project is worth 30% of your grade. If you did well, keep up the good work! If you would like to have done better, focus in on the Case Project worth 45%, and the remaining classes for class participation.

Conclusion

The teaching profession is one of lifelong learning. The hands-on, action-oriented tools and tips that are provided in this book will help you to succeed as you begin your journey toward teaching excellence. The **At a Glance** summaries in each chapter will enable you to refer back easily to this book and focus in on the areas of teaching that are most pertinent to you as you continue on this exciting journey.

Over time, you will evolve as a teacher and will continue to learn, not only from resources such as this book, but also from your colleagues, your students, and from your own successes and mistakes along the way. As your teaching evolves, be patient with yourself and take the opportunity to experiment with new approaches. Don't worry if you stumble now and then. Your students will appreciate your efforts and will be surprisingly supportive if you're passionate and enthusiastic about your teaching.

Indeed, passion and enthusiasm will drive your ability to deliver a course that not only stimulates and engages your students, but also inspires them. As business instructors, we have the unique opportunity to impact the people who will influence the business world of the future. Use this book to help you teach courses that create a positive impact that extends long beyond the last class.

INDEX